Abominable Firebug

Abominable Firebug

Richard B. Johnson
Engineer, Commercial Pilot,
Musician, and Inventor

iUniverse, Inc.
New York Lincoln Shanghai

Abominable Firebug

iUniverse books may be ordered through booksellers or by contacting:

iUniverse
2021 Pine Lake Road, Suite 100
Lincoln, NE 68512
www.iuniverse.com
1-800-Authors (1-800-288-4677)

ISBN-13: 978-0-595-38667-3 (pbk)
ISBN-13: 978-0-595-83047-3 (ebk)
ISBN-10: 0-595-38667-9 (pbk)
ISBN-10: 0-595-83047-1 (ebk)

Printed in the United States of America

Contents

Foreword

I read this extraordinary book through the critical lenses of teacher, clinician, and professor. My twenty-three-year professional career has been dedicated to educating students similar to those described in these pages, and training the teachers and administrators who work in the schools these students attend.

I do have another interest in this book, however. The author, Richard B. "Dick" Johnson, is my neighbor in a small, sleepy, suburban town in Massachusetts. My children have grown up listening to the mischievous stories of the "Bad Momber." Dick joins us for evening coffee, Christmas morning, holiday meals, and lengthy, heated discussions of local Yankee politics. He might be characterized as anyone's average neighbor next door. However, I would never use the descriptor "average" in the same sentence with Dick's name. He is brilliant—a genius I suspect—although I have no quantitative proof. As you the reader will know from reading the account of his early life, Dick's life experiences were far from average.

This book will reveal the appalling realities of the juvenile detention system. At the same time, however, this book will give you hope. It is clear that mentors made a grand difference in Richard B. Johnson's life. Dick succeeded *in spite* of his gruesome experiences. *You* can learn from this autobiography and become a better teacher, clinician, probation officer, or counselor. *You* can understand that behavior is an expression of feelings that cannot be expressed in words. *You* can have hope that the kids that are not the easiest to care for or understand can and do grow up to be successful adults with the guidance of dedicated adult mentors. *You* can take it upon yourself to reach out to these kids in a meaningful manner.

Perhaps you are a professor evaluating this book as a potential required text for a course you teach. Perhaps you are a student of social work, criminal justice, counseling, or teaching. Through the aforementioned lenses of authoritative understanding, I found several significant themes emerge:

1. Dick's total love of his family despite their rejection

2. The resiliency of youth

viii   Abominable Firebug

3.   The need to be loved and important to others

4.   The role of mentors, and

5.   The manner in which a reputation follows a person over years

These five themes are essential for human service workers to understand, so that they can better serve the clients with whom they work. This amazing, descriptive work sets the scene for understanding these critical themes.

Despite Dick's horrific experiences, he would be considered a highly successful adult when held against any standard. As an accomplished engineer, he has developed sophisticated, complex systems. That requires dedication, persistence, intelligence, and tenacity. He is well-read, well-informed, and extremely interesting. He is a pilot, plumber, electrician, mechanic, musician, and carpenter. He has a great love and affinity for fixing things. He is kind to people in need.

Dick is an inspiration. By capturing his experiences on paper for all to read, he breathes new hope into the desperate lives of disaffected youth. Dick gives a loud voice to many who have remained silent.

Whether a professional caregiver, parent, or friend of youth at risk, we owe it to all these children to share the knowledge we gain from Dick's book. Read this book and share it with others. Open people's eyes to the harsh realities of those children locked and tossed away, and share their worth and potential.

Dr. Mary A. Clisbee, Executive Director, Merrimack Special Education Collaborative, Massachusetts.

Acknowledgments

Reviewers:
  Dr. John B. Barranco
  Rev. F. Robert Brown
  Dr. Mary A. Clisbee
  Rich Wood

Art and photography:
  Richard B. Johnson
  William Siy Tin

The Runaway:
  Anthony Clisbee

Copy Editor:
  Nowick Gray

Preface

If I were a famous person, writing a story about my childhood would be very easy. People want to read about famous people. However, this is a story about the ordinary person who lived next door—well, maybe not too ordinary…

Growing up in the late fifties and early sixties, I was a resident of two foster home institutions, a detention center, and a two-time inmate of a reform school. It is not a pretty picture, but a story that should be told. This is not the story of a loser. I eventually graduated from college. As an electronics engineer, I designed electronic equipment ranging from radio transmitters used around the world, also equipment used for nuclear magnetic resonance applications and CAT scanners. I also have a commercial pilot's license and fly my own airplane.

This story is true. Nothing has been changed to create a story line. This is mostly a history about the Massachusetts Youth Service Board and the Lyman School for Boys.

When I first knew I was going to be confined to a reform school, I was frightened that I might be hurt by the other inmates. These fears turned out to have no basis in fact. As a resident of Lyman School, I was one of many who "never had it so good." However, it was the tortuous road I traveled to get there that was most painful, but nonetheless interesting.

This book is dedicated to Mark D. Devlin, author of *Stubborn Child,* who, starting at the age of seven, took the same path through the Massachusetts Juvenile Court System as I did. He did not survive, dying as a homeless alcoholic at the age of fifty-six. He was destroyed by the Massachusetts Juvenile Court System, having never committed a crime before entering its custody.

1

My Home

During World War II, my father worked as a plater for a company in Worcester, Massachusetts. He became a foreman on the line and a self-taught chemist. I am going to write a bit about my father and his contributions, so you can understand something about my background. In addition, some of the things that I write about may seem rather tech-nical, but bear with me, this whole book was written by a high school dropout, so it should be an easy read.

The company was a government contractor, asked to try to silver-plate aluminum for use in combat radios, man pack, and tank. The existing radios were very heavy because they used a silver-plated copper chassis. New technology had brought VHF to these radios. It allowed for shorter antennas, greater range, and reduced interference. This technology, however, required that the radios be constructed using a silver-plated chassis. If the company could find a way to silver-plate aluminum, the weight and cost of these radios would be much reduced. Previous attempts to plate aluminum had not been successful. As soon as the aluminum was put into a plating bath, it was attacked and turned black. It was commonplace to start the plating of all common metals by plating copper first. Copper was inexpensive, filled in many voids, and created an ideal base for subsequent plating of the final product, such as silver or chrome plating.

1

When my father learned about the failed experiments to plate aluminum, he asked his boss if he could try. His boss told him that he could have access to the shop after normal working hours or on weekends if he could clear it with the security guards. My father would often eat lunch with a security guard, so obtaining access was no problem. Anyway, my father started to investigate how to copper-plate and then silver-plate aluminum. My father learned that if you take a piece of aluminum that had become corroded by immersing it in copper sulfate, a plating bath, and then immerse it in a strong acid like nitric or sulfuric acid, the corrosion would be cleaned off. Therefore, he reasoned, if he added just the right amount of sulfuric acid to the copper sulfate so that the rate at which it was being corroded equaled the rate at which it was being cleaned, he would be successful in plating the aluminum. In fact, he was successful, and he proudly presented his boss with a silver-plated aluminum radio chassis on the following Monday morning.

That was how my father became an inventor after a single weekend of experimentation. My grandfather was an inventor too. He invented shackle bolts, those U-shaped things that connect leaf springs to axles on trucks and automobiles. For my father's invention, he received a few hundred dollars, enough money to make a small down payment on some land in North Brookfield, Massachusetts. The land was near a cemetery on Elm Street and supported an old barn. He decided to convert the barn to a house. To start with, my father built a small shack clad with tarpaper where he, my mother, my eldest sister, and I could stay on the weekends while he was working on the house. I was born a short time before my father started working on the house. The house was never really completed. It was always undergoing some kind of renovation. Nevertheless, it was sufficient for my father and mother to raise a family. After the war ended, my father lost his factory job. He then decided to become a sales representative. He sold home improvement items such as storm windows, aluminum awnings, fire extinguishers, asbestos siding, and lightning rods.

The house did not have any electricity until well after I started middle school. In fact, it did not even have running water. My parents and my older sister would cart water from a faucet in the cemetery. One of my first chores was to fill the stove with kerosene from a drum in the backyard. My sisters' chores involved filling the kerosene lamps and trimming their wicks.

Eventually my father installed running water by burying pipe for over a quarter of a mile to connect with the town water supply on Ward Street. Even though this work was done by hand, we never had that feed-line freeze. My father knew that once you are committed to do some work, you must do it correctly, so he buried that long pipe well below the frost line.

Later on, my father installed a gravity-fed furnace so that the house could be heated with lower-cost fuel oil. Nevertheless, we continued to use the kerosene stove for cooking and to heat water for our weekly baths. Bath time was Saturday night whether we needed it or not! We all shared the same bathwater. My mother would fill a large tub on the kitchen floor and warm its water from some boiled on the stove. First, she would give my younger sister a bath. Then my older sister would take her bath. Then it was my turn. After all the children had taken their baths, my parents would send us off to bed and take their baths.

In time, my older sister became too mature to take a bath on the kitchen floor. It was then that my father finally installed electricity and an electric water heater. My family was probably one of the last families to obtain electricity in North Brookfield. This had been put off as long as possible because the electric company required that my father pay for an electric light pole. The cost of that pole was greater than the cost of the whole house, my father said.

We were all used to being without electricity. My grandparents' home in Marathon, New York, never had electricity. In fact, I was told that nobody on my grandparents' street had electricity because there was gas street lighting and natural gas was fed to all the homes.

I well remember the day, some ten years after my father began building the house, when I came home from school for lunch and the battery radio was broadcasting the news about Sputnik. My father proudly reached up from the kitchen table and switched on a circular florescent light.

Eventually the battery radio disappeared, replaced with a Zenith Trans-Oceanic console radio with a band switch for listening to shortwave as well as regular broadcasts. With electricity came my father's amateur radio station. His call sign was WN1CJO. He set up a little area on an all-weather porch he built to communicate with the world using Morse code. Eventually I obtained an amateur radio license as well, although I was never allowed to use my father's equipment.

As a child, I was given more and more work to do as I became older and more physically capable. I not only did the barn work but also the yard work as well. My mother enforced some very strict rules of conduct. If I did not come home from school at the appropriate time, I was whipped. My mother seemed to be extremely afraid that I would somehow hurt my two sisters. Detecting this, my youngest sister would take advantage of this during situations of normal sibling rivalry by accusing me of hitting her, or otherwise causing her problems. This would result in whippings, basement detention, and other punishments.

My mother was readily enraged. She would fly into a screaming tirade upon the slightest provocation. My father, however, was always quite reserved and protective.

For instance, when I was learning to walk at about two years of age, I would carry things around that would seem to provide support. My little sister learned to walk by carrying around a rubber boot. I was more daring and used a milk bottle! One day I stepped off the terrace into midair. It wasn't so much the flight that bothered me, but the landing with the milk bottle in my hand. My mother started screaming at me as my father picked me up and started wiping the blood from my head and face. I had just completed my first flight lesson, and this wasn't going to be a good day. My father rushed me to the doctor's office in Spencer, Massachusetts. He ran about a mile and a half to Varney's gas station on State Route 9 in town, where a bus would stop within the hour and take us to Spencer. Dr. O'Boyle stitched me up and, in a few days, I was as good as new.

I wanted my mother to hold me in her arms and comfort me. I hurt where the doctor had stitched my head and arm. Instead, my mother punished me by making me go to bed without any supper. This was the very first punishment I remember.

I was never able to understand my mother, nor she me! She seemed to assume that there was some hidden agenda in every act of kindness. Of course, I was naïve. I would eventually learn that there were people out there who did have more transparent agendas.

My mother instituted rules that were unlike the rules shared by my classmates. For instance, I was not allowed to enter the house except through the basement. I was never allowed in the living room except to clean it, and then only under close supervision. I could enter the kitchen only for meals or for cleaning the floor. I was never allowed to eat anything except what was put onto my plate during those meals. My family had a telephone before we had electricity. I was never allowed to use that phone.

My two sisters were exempt from these rules. They could use anything they wanted and they could come and go as they pleased. They shared a large room. I lived in a tiny alcove under the slope of the roof at the top of the stairs. Most of the space was taken by the stairwell so my actual living space was only large enough for a modified army cot. Eventually I would claim some space below the stairs to keep my treasures such as boxes of old radio tubes I had rescued from trash barrels in town. Initially, this room didn't even have a window. This was because the ceiling sloped nearly to the floor. Eventually my father found a window that was small enough to install in that space. It contained a single pane of glass. This allowed me to lie on the floor and watch the sunset through my private window. Compared to my room, my sisters' room was huge. Before I started school, I thought this favoritism towards girls was normal. After all, girls could hit you, but you could not hit them back. After I found out that other boys were not treated as I was, I became somewhat of a problem for my mother.

One time I went to the house of a friend, Tom Falls, after school. I was surprised that he brought me in through the front door of his house. I had never been allowed to enter the front door of my house. I had to use the basement door and climb up the basement stairs into a storage area beneath the stairs, remove my shoes, then continue up to my room. After Tom brought me into the living room, he had me sit on the couch. I was never allowed to sit on the couch in my parents' living room! Then he went into the kitchen and "stole" (I figured) some sandwiches and some milk. I was sure that he would be greatly punished if his parents found out. He gave me a glass of milk and a sandwich. Always hungry, I started to wolf down the sandwich, until Tom's mother appeared in the doorway. I tried to hide the food. I sat on the sandwich!

The grade school in North Brookfield was called the "Yellow School." It was a four-room wooden structure near the Fire Station. It contained a boiler room in the rear, which also housed the toilet facilities. We were taught to raise our hand, one finger or two, to get the teacher's permission to use the toilet. This building overlooked a dirt schoolyard on School Street. A railroad track ran along the northeast side of Elm Street and both wyed with School Street approaching the center of town.

Across the street from the school was one of the town's major employers, the "The Asbestos Shop." This company, the Aztec Industries Asbestos Textile Company, made asbestos cloth as well as other asbestos products. Raw asbestos was delivered to the factory in open railroad cars. As schoolchildren, we played with this material, stripping away the fibers and watching them float in the air. We were taught that asbestos was an inert mineral. Being inert, it was probably one of the safest toys around. The company would grind and fluff the asbestos, then spin it into a thread. The thread would be supplied to the looms to make cloth. When the grinders and fluffers were running, the entire schoolyard and most of the town would be covered with asbestos fibers, as if from a light snowfall. There was some talk around town about starting a wet process to cut down on the amount of escaping fibers, but the cost of the water was thought to be too great. As schoolchildren, we went on supervised visits to the factory several times. Of course, many boys, me included, would wander into the factory during lunch period or recess. It was a fascinating place to visit. We are probably all now destined to die of mesothelioma.

Just down the street was another factory, Quabaug Rubber, affectionately called "the Rubber Shop." This factory produced natural rubber items like shoe soles and military raincoats. Many dry chemicals such as carbon black, sulfur, red lead oxide, and natural rubber, in large bundles that looked like hams, were delivered in both open and closed railroad cars. Some of these railroad cars displayed warning signs: "Do not hump." It was one of these signs that piqued my imagination enough to wonder what "hump" meant. I started to read about trains and often dreamed of becoming a railroad engineer. During recess, we would play in those cars, sometimes being covered with black or red pigment. Red lead was considered to be simply a paint pigment, messy but harmless. Children were taught never to chew on painted items anyway, so such materials were not considered hazardous at all! Both carbon black and red lead often covered the street near the school, having been deposited from the occasional broken paper sacks as the railcars were being unloaded.

The railroad track ran from downtown North Brookfield to East Brookfield. It was only a single track spur, so the train needed to go backwards all the way to East Brookfield. On its way, it passed by my family's house. Early on, the railroad engine was a steam engine fed by coal. Later, a steam engine fed by oil pulled the train. Eventually a more modern diesel electric locomotive pulled it.

I lived about a mile from school. According to school department rules, the school bus was available for students who lived over a mile away. I was never allowed to ride the bus even when I attended middle school on Grove Street because I lived less than a mile away, depending upon who measured it, and what they were attempting to prove. Recent measurements show that I lived over a mile away, but that is probably because of universe expansion. Simply stated, nobody in authority wanted me to ride the bus. There were many excuses. The strangest interpretation of the bus-distance rule occurred when my younger sister started school. She was able to ride the bus. I was not.

Anyway, it was much more enjoyable to walk along the railroad tracks. Sometimes as I was walking, the train would come by. I would step off the tracks and let the slow-moving freighter pass by. I would wave to the engineer and often he would wave back. One day the train stopped and the engineer beckoned me to come aboard the engine. When the train stopped in front of the schoolyard, I was very proud as I stepped off that train in front of my schoolmates.

The Yellow School housed first to fourth grades. Nobody in North Brookfield attended kindergarten in those days, so we all started out the same. We only knew the "no" words and could not read, write, or carry on a conversation. By the time we entered the second grade, though, we were able to converse and had started to read. After completing the fourth grade, every child was able to read, write, exercise penmanship, and perform day-to-day mathematical operations such as making change.

Many of my classmates were of Polish extraction. Their parents spoke Polish and retained it as a "secret" language. The children all spoke English. Many did not understand what their parents were saying in their native tongue. That allowed their parents the opportunity to converse without the children knowing what the grown-ups were saying.

We were to stand by our desks and recite from a book while learning to read. I found it very difficult to read. In fact, I even had a speech impediment that made me stutter. As I would stand to read, my classmates would jeer. This became very embarrassing. In grade school, we did not have school homework, but I asked my teacher if I could take the book home to study it. She agreed, so I asked her what paragraph she would have me read the following day. She picked out a paragraph.

At home, after my chores, I studied that paragraph. I practiced pronouncing every word. I even paused for the punctuation marks. I was ready for my big event; I would show everybody that I could read.

The following day, during recitation, Walter Lee read my paragraph! Walter was the class know-it-all; his father owned the "Red Lee Construction Company." When it was my turn, I could not read and cried, "Walter read my paragraph!" The teacher said, "Yes. Sit down! You may never learn to read." So I felt like a total failure. Walter could read, I could only cry.

After chores that day, I went to my room and memorized the whole book. On the following Monday we had recitation again. When it came time for me to read, I slowly rose to my feet. I took two steps forward to plant my feet squarely by the side of my desk. I picked up the book, held it in my left hand by its spine, used my right index finger to mark my place, and then began to recite.

I read the whole page without any mistakes. I turned and sat back down. Silence filled the classroom. I looked towards the teacher and she was wiping tears from her eyes. Then, after the longest pause, practically everybody started to cheer except, of course, Walter Lee. I had read his paragraph!

I still could not speak without stuttering. That became a problem. I wanted to show that I was just as smart as everybody else was so that my classmates would not exclude me from playing with them. Once I learned to read I discovered that if I wrote the things down that I wanted to say, and then read them back, I would not stutter. I started to carry scraps of paper so I could write what I wanted to say.

Eventually I learned to write things down in my "mind's eye" and then read them back. This eliminated the problem with paper and, incidentally, helped me speak with much more grammatical correctness than many of my classmates.

By the time I was in middle school, I could speak with no hint of a stutter and with a correctness that made me the envy of many classmates. I planned to become a radio announcer. Right now, I just wanted to become an amateur radio operator and talk to the world!

In the early evening, after a hot June day in 1953, at the age of ten, I was walking home from a Grange meeting in North Brookfield. All of us farm boys were required to attend the Grange, where we learned how to plant corn and potatoes in straight rows and not complain when our parents required us to hoe those rows. As I looked to the sky towards Worcester, I saw a gigantic mushroom-shaped cloud. Its surface would occasionally flash with bright lightning, visible even though the setting sun illuminated the cloud. I had never seen a cloud like this before. The cloud reached so high into the sky that the top was not visible, even though the sky around it was clear blue. This was the famous Worcester tornado as seen from twenty miles away.

When I got home, my mother was terrified. She thought that the Russians had bombed Worcester. She had seen mushroom-shaped clouds in the pictures of atomic tests. The electric power and the telephones were off in the neighborhood and there were no batteries for the portable radio. My father had not installed electricity in the house yet, so my mother knew only what the neighbors could tell her. Since I had just walked a mile or so, exposed to the elements, she was afraid that I would track radiation into the house, so I had to remain in the basement. Eventually I was allowed out of the basement, but not until my father returned home and assured my mother that I could not have tracked any radiation into the house that could hurt her girls.

My father had been canvassing in the Worcester area, so it took him a long time to return home. He had to use his car as a tractor to push some broken branches off a highway so he could return. Also, hail had pelted the car, so there were dents practically all over it. After this trip, my father decided that it was time to trade in his used Hudson to get his first new car, a Nash Rambler. He also decided to get the family a television set so we could be better informed and prepared for emergencies.

My father did not intend to allow anybody in his family to while away their time watching one of those things just for kicks. Nevertheless, he decided that, for educational purposes only, it was time to get a television set. Of course, he had to install electricity first. Incidentally, since he was in the home improvement business, he knew that there would be windfall profits resulting from the Worcester tornado.

I had other adventures while walking to and from school. One day I found a wallet containing eight dollars. It contained a driver's license as well, so I took the money and deposited the wallet into a mailbox. I spent the money on a fountain pen and lots of candy. I would not have been caught except for a girl named Sybil. She was the class tomboy who got her kicks by beating up boys. She knew that boys would not hit her back, so she would seriously hurt them. Anyway, when she found that I was sharing candy with others, but not her, she told the teacher that I must have stolen the candy. The teacher and future principal, Miss Ruby A. O'Coin, confronted me and actually beat me severely until I told her about the wallet. She used corporal punishment on many students. Her favorite punishment was to use a special ruler, which was 18 inches in length, but very thick and triangular, to administer her blows to our outstretched hands. Failure to keep the hands outstretched would result in a slap to the face, although not with the ruler. In this case, she kept slamming me against the cloakroom wall until I was bleeding from my nose and was so senseless that I told her what I had done. Sybil looked on and laughed.

Miss O'Coin reported my "theft" to my mother. Neither thought that the adage "Finders keepers; losers weepers" had any merit. My mother was, as usual, livid! She whipped me so badly that my legs swelled and became black and blue. For many weeks, I could barely walk to school. I was about eight years of age at the time. Highly respected by most of the students' parents, most of the students, including my older sister, hated Miss O'Coin.

Some adventures during my schoolhouse walk actually turned out quite well. When I was about ten years old, I found a wooden box that had apparently fallen off a truck. It was very heavy and it took me a long time to drag it along the street and into the schoolyard. I called a teacher (not Miss O'Coin, by the way) and asked her what I should do. She read the label and called the owner from the school telephone. The owner and, as it turned out, the sender was Mr. Frank Cook, the founder of Cook Optics in town. When he arrived to pick it up, he said that it was a very expensive instrument and there were probably only two or three in the whole world. He wanted to give me five dollars for taking care of it. I told him my mother would not let me have any money, but my father could probably use the money instead. I am unsure of any connection, but Mr. Cook eventually gave my father a job.

2

The Piano

In the forties, when an elder family member was dying, they would plan the event and, at the last moment, call all the family members together for a last farewell. Children and grandchildren would come from all around the country, gather around the dying elder's bed, be given many kisses and blessings, and then overnight the elder would expire into  some wondrous sleep called "passed away." Such was the case with Great-Grandmother Watrous.

I was about two years old when my father learned that his grandmother was dying, he packed the family into his Packard panel truck and set off on the hazardous journey across the Berkshire Mountains to Marathon, New York, in the dead of winter. The truck had a worn transmission, so my father had attached a screen-door spring between the gearshift lever and the springs under the front seat. This was to keep the machine from popping out of gear. The heater did not work, so as we started up the Mohawk Trail, we began to shiver even though we were all wrapped up with blankets. At the top of the mountain, near a small village called Florida, the truck had run out of water, so my father had to melt some snow to put into the radiator. Such was the adventure during my first trip to New York State, which took nearly twenty-four hours.

After recovering from the trip at my grandfather's home in Marathon for several days, we went to my great-grandmother's house, and I saw this monstrous, magical machine in her living room. It was the first piano I had ever seen. While climbing onto the piano bench, I tipped it over. Some music charts fell out because I did not know that the top would open up. A second try was more successful, and I started to play Mozart, Rachmaninoff, and Bach on the piano. At least, that is what my impromptu audience said it was. Anyway, my parents were told that I had a great "gift," that I would become a great piano player. Thus began the horror of piano lessons and many more failed expectations.

After my great-grandmother's funeral, my father brought that piano two hundred fifty miles back across the Berkshire Hills in the back of the panel truck, with the children wedged in as well. At home, it was installed onto a porch that was promptly boarded up to make it a four-season room, cold in the winter, and sweltering in the summer. This would become my piano prison for sometime to come.

Nobody ever asked me if I wanted to become a pianist. It was just assumed that I had some God-given gift and it would be some kind of horrific sin if I did not use that gift. When I was eight years old, my parents found several cheap piano teachers for me.

During my grade school years, the town Grange put on several "Talent Scout" shows where parents forced their children to come before an audience of strangers and attempt to play instruments or sing songs.

When my time came, I would sit at an out-of-tune piano and attempt to play something from the *John Thompson* piano lesson book *du jour*. I always got mild claps from a few elders and jeers from my classmates. The winners were often kids who played the spoons or sang popular songs off-key—the children of town officials.

This was not what you would call positive reinforcement. Nevertheless, my parents forced me to continue, and by the time I entered middle school, the school had a music teacher. The music teacher also thought that I had promise, so he spent considerable time and effort trying to teach me to play the piano.

At school we had some talent shows as well. The shows were not contests, so there were no winners or losers—except, perhaps, the music teacher. These shows were largely designed to show that the music teacher was performing well. The principal would call an assembly; all the students filed into the hall and sat and listened to auditions from soon-to-be high school band players and a few unfortunates like myself who played non-band instruments.

Again, it became my time to make a fool of myself. I sat down at the piano and began to play Franz Liszt's *Liebesträume*, "Dream of Love." My classmates started to yell and jeer. I slammed down the keyboard cover and stormed off the stage.

Mr. Thompson, the music teacher, grabbed me by the neck, shook me, and said, "I didn't spend my goddamn time teaching you so you could make a fool of me. Now, you go back out there, play it, and play it right." I walked back out onto the stage and played the piece. The audience was silent at first. Then, as I walked off the stage, the room came to life. There were no jeers, only a thunderous applause. From the back of the room started a cadence, "More, more, more..." More learned children probably would have said, "Encore..."

I went back to the piano and played Elvis Presley's *Love Me Tender*. This was a new popular song in 1956. Nobody ever jeered when I played the piano again. Oh! If my mother had caught me playing a song I heard on the radio, I would have been punished. I played it by ear, never having played it before.

3

Amateur Radio Operator

When I started middle school, I tried to make some friends, but I was rejected at every turn. It seemed that nobody wanted to associate with someone who smelled like goat manure and was unable to stay around and play after school.

I lived on a small farm where we raised chickens and goats. The goats were a pain in the butt (pun intended). Every night after school, I would go home and clean the barn. I always smelled like goat manure. About once a month, I had to clean the chicken house. During the spring and summer months I kept the garden weeded and hoed. This continual work isolated me from my peers. I had very little time to play and was never allowed to go to somebody else's house. There were times that I would sneak off and go exploring, but I was always in trouble with my parents when I returned.

I met an older person who had just started high school. He said he was an amateur radio operator and was able to communicate with people all over the world, just like my father. He said he had an advanced class license, worked all the bands, and ran a kilowatt rig on the 75-meter phone band. He used all the ham radio lingo and I was quite impressed. His house was near the top of a hill called Mount Guyot, so I expected that he probably could communicate with just about anybody in the world. Although he had a large number of antennas at his house, he would not let me see his radio station until I got at least a novice amateur radio license. He said that was a rule set by his father, who was with the Secret Service.

To be just like him, I started to study to get an amateur radio license. The technical theory was easy. I could just read that from books. However, the Morse code part was harder, because I needed to listen to somebody sending code, and I needed to send code to somebody who could receive it and verify its accuracy.

Learning Morse code is very difficult when you are all alone. My family had the Zenith Trans-Oceanic shortwave radio, but my mother would not let me listen to it because it was in the forbidden living room. Furthermore, the shortwave code on that radio was just ship-to-shore from experienced radiotelegraph operators who sent code at 50 to 60 words per minute. I could never copy that. I needed to learn five words per minute first.

I had started a paper route. I did not make much money, because I had many customers who would not pay. They would claim that they had gotten only half their papers, so they would only pay me only half the price. The problem was that I had to pay the paper company the full price. Often, at the end of the week I had earned only two or three dollars. Furthermore, my mother required that I put all the money in a savings account. I was not allowed to waste money by buying nonessentials. Nevertheless, the paper route was not a complete waste of time. I met customers and others who could help me. One customer, Mr. Dupree, worked in the Rubber Shop. He had an old Hallicrafters shortwave radio that was just sitting in his garage. I asked him if I could have it. He said, "Sure!"

I took the radio home and my mother met me at the cellar door. She was sure that I had stolen it. When I told her that Mr. Dupree had given it to me, she screamed that I had been selling my body to the lowest bidder. I had no clue as to what she was talking about. She beat me severely and tried to smash up the radio. I covered the radio with my body, but she tore it away and threw it into the cesspool. Yes, we had a cesspool in our backyard. One had to be careful not to fall in because it was only covered with loose planks.

When my father came home from work, he asked where I had gotten the radio. I told him that Mr. Dupree had given it to me. He asked why Mr. Dupree had given it to me and I responded, "Because I asked for it." Anyway, my father fished the radio out of the cesspool and washed it off with a garden hose. I carefully removed all the tubes and cleaned out everything. This took several hours of patient work. The loudspeaker was destroyed, but I would get one from the TV repair shop in town another day. After the radio dried out, I replaced the loudspeaker and it worked.

To use the radio, I needed to make a longwire antenna. My father already had an antenna, but I could not use that. There was no money for me to buy the 150 feet or so of wire and some insulators needed to support the antenna. I needed to find someone who would give me some wire. I asked the TV repairman, the electrical contractor, and the telephone company if I could have some wire for an antenna. Nobody would give me any. In addition, I noted that the used wire that the electrical contractor had rolled up and stored behind his shop was suddenly cut into little pieces. He certainly did not want me to make an antenna.

Next, I went over to the apple orchard, Lincoln Orchard, later to be named Brookfield Orchards, and talked to the owner, Mr. Hamilton "Hammy" Lincoln. He said that he had an electric fence that needed to be taken down and I could have the wire if I took it down for him. I took it down, piled all the steel posts in the right place, rolled up the wire, and took it home. Again, my mother was furious. She was sure that I had stolen the electric fence wire from somebody's pasture. She got out her switch and started beating me. I was getting very angry. I grabbed the switch from her hands and broke it into four pieces. Then I threw the handful of sticks at her and walked away. She kept yelling and screaming, "Wait until your father gets home. You'll be sorry!" She locked me out of the house.

When my father came home from work, he asked what had happened. I told him that Hammy Lincoln said I could have the wire if I took down his fence. My father drove over to the orchard and talked to Mr. Lincoln. He came back with the metal fence posts in the back of his car. Mr. Lincoln had given him the rest of the fence!

Now I had to help my father install the fence. It would be used as a corral for the goats when the barn was being cleaned. He told me, "We'll run a strand over to the side of the house so you can use it as an antenna when the goats are not in the corral." It worked fine. The corral was never actually used for the goats because my father did not want to buy an electric fence charger. In fact, my father's intention all along was that it would be a cleverly disguised shortwave antenna.

I used that radio to listen to code on the novice bands and I was able to listen to the ARRL (American Radio Relay League) code classes as well. Eventually I was confident enough to take my amateur radio license test. My father drove me to West Brookfield to an extra-class amateur radio operator, Mr. Charles "Charley" Tamn. He administered the test, and I became a technician class amateur radio operator, bypassing the novice license entirely. My father remained a novice. I detected a certain pride in my father's voice when he told my mother and sisters that I had become an amateur radio operator of a class more advanced than his.

I rummaged through trash barrels behind the TV repair shop trying to find some components to make a radio transmitter and a converter so I could transmit and receive on the six-meter amateur radio band. I was never able to get anything working, mostly because I did not have the tools or the patience to complete the projects I started.

I did get to go on the air, at weekly Civil Defense meetings at the firehouse in East Brookfield. That is where I found out that the person in school who had said he was an amateur radio operator was no such thing. He did not have the call letters he claimed to have, and in fact, at the time, my father and I were the only two radio amateurs in North Brookfield. This bothered me quite a bit, because I had wanted to be just like this so-called amateur radio operator. I had worked so hard to be just like him. He seemed so smart; everybody liked him, and he looked like a movie star. Now I had found out that he was a liar. I wondered if his father had really been in the Secret Service. Maybe he was a spy, using all those antennas! Or maybe not—if he were a real spy, he would have used an electric fence.

At another time, in another place, I would build and operate an amateur radio station. It would become a window, obtaining unexpected freedom from an unexpected place.

4

The First Fire

I was not a very good student as a freshman at North Brookfield High, but I had a fascinating chemistry teacher, Mr. Dahlquist. One of his demonstrations used white phosphorus dissolved in carbon disulphide. He would pour a small quantity of this substance onto a piece of filter paper, and as soon as the solvent evaporated, the paper would burst  into flames. This stuff was neat! After class, I appropriated a small quantity of the substance and proceeded to make paper towels mysteriously burst into flames in the men's room. I gave what was left to a friend and went on to class. About ten minutes later, the fire bell rang and I became aware that this was not a fire drill! Someone had set a trash container on fire in the janitor's closet near the men's room.

There was an investigation. The chief of police, Mr. DeLude, investigated, and I became a suspect in that investigation. I told him that I knew nothing about the fire. I also told him that I had been experimenting with the substance in the men's room, since I knew that many students had seen me playing with the chemicals, so it was fruitless to try to cover up. I mentioned that I was probably not the only one who was playing with the substance, but I never told him to whom I gave the chemicals. I was suspended from school for two weeks.

Part of my punishment at home involved sleeping in the barn with the animals. This became the ultimate of all punishments. I even wished that I were dead. I made up my mind that I would never again ever go through something like that.

I dreamed about running away. I did not know where I would go, or what I would do when I got to wherever it was that I was going, but I dreamed about going to the city. To me, the city was some far away place like Worcester. Worcester held all the promises and dreams of a new life and adventure. Somehow, I felt that I had to justify running away. I did not know that people often run away for no reason at all! I was only fourteen years of age.

When I returned to school, I was warned that I was being watched. I was on probation. "The only reason I am letting you return," said Mr. Leach, the school principal, "is because we don't have enough evidence to prosecute you." Mr. Leach was an extremely abusive person. It seemed as though he got his rocks off by physically abusing children. He had hit me on the top of my head with his knuckles several times for minor infractions of rules, which were being continually created out of midair. These he called "noogies."

I did not like being threatened. I knew that I had not set the fire, and I even thought of myself as a hero for not finking on the person who might have. I stayed in school for another week before being kicked out for good. What got me kicked out was a trick I had learned from a classmate. If you take a ballpoint pen and draw a circle around the knuckle of your index finger, then draw a line halfway through that circle, you can cradle that knuckle in your other hand in such a way that it looks as though you have exposed your penis. I showed this trick to several girls in the homeroom class. Actually, I showed this trick to just about everybody and I don't really think that anybody thought that I had actually exposed myself, but I was promptly dismissed from class and from North Brookfield High forever!

Prepared for being kicked out of school, I came to class with my savings account passbook. I went directly to the bank and withdrew the entire balance of thirty-seven dollars that I had earned on my paper route. The bank wanted to check with my parents, but I convinced the teller that this was for a wedding anniversary gift, and that she would ruin the whole thing by calling my folks.

5

Running Away

I had a bicycle, but it was broken. It had been broken for over a year. The bicycle broke when I was riding down Walnut Street and a truck backed out into my path. I hit the back of the truck and flew into its bed. The truck driver got out, swore at me, then pulled me off his truck and tossed my bicycle and me off to the side of the road. He handled me like I was a sack of garbage. I felt very lucky that he did not claim that I damaged his truck. Anyway, the forks were broken, so I did not have a bicycle to ride anymore. If I was going to run away to the big city, I had to hitchhike.

Off I went up the Oakham Road towards Paxton. I thought that I would have a better chance of getting a ride on the back road and less of a chance of being picked up by the police. The distance from North Brookfield to Paxton was nearly fifteen miles. I walked that entire distance. On the common in Paxton was a church. This church was having a Halloween party, where they were serving cider and donuts. I was hungry.

I invited myself to the party and filled up on cider and donuts. While other partygoers were bobbing for apples and playing other party games, I went into the sanctuary where the lights were off and lay down on a pew to get some sleep.

The first rape

The sound of the party slowly quieted as the church members went home. I thought I was alone as I drifted off to sleep. Suddenly I was awakened by the touch of a hand upon my private parts. A man with a cleric's collar stood before me and fumbled with the zipper on my pants. I opened only one eye slightly, feigning sleep. He slowly dropped to his knees and sucked my penis into his mouth. He made some moaning sounds as I felt his teeth against sensitive skin. I was frightened and felt trapped. I did nothing, just barely breathing; I waited as if for certain death. With a sigh, the man quietly left. My private parts were sore.

I sat alone in the church, in the dark, wondering what would happen next. What had happened? I was confused and bewildered, and I asked myself many questions. In a while, the police arrived. What were the police doing here? How did they know I was here? I knew I was trapped. I could only pretend to be asleep in the pews and be discovered during the police search.

"What are you doing here?" demanded a voice behind a bright flashlight. "What's your name? Where did you come from?" The police took me to the station and telephoned my parents. Now I was in real bad trouble. To this day, I believe that the minister who raped me in God's sanctuary completed the job by calling the police and telling them I was hiding in the church. So much for religion!

Several weeks passed. My life at home was the most miserable one could imagine. I was confined to the barn. I was frightened on several occasions by rats that crawled into my pockets while I was asleep in the barn. Before, I had slept on some hay in the corner away from the draft. It was now late autumn and the draft was very cold. Between the rats and the cold, I decided to sleep at the side of my favorite goat. Her name was Manny. She was a Toggenburg crossbreed, brown in color, with a white pattern on her side that looked like the Big Dipper. I slept with my head on the Big Dipper.

Since there were laws in Massachusetts that required one to attend school until the age of sixteen, and since I was neither sixteen, nor attending school, my parents tried to get me "sent up" somewhere so I would no longer be a problem for them. To this end, they enlisted the aid of a psychologist in the outpatient department of Worcester Memorial Hospital.

The first thing I did was take a complete set of tests. These involved everything from the basic IQ tests, inkblot tests, and interactive communications tests to the more complex tests of brain function like the electroencephalograph. There was nothing much wrong with me that could be found from a purely clinical point of view. I had an exceptionally high IQ, so I was told, and my other responses were perfectly normal. "Why is it, then," said the psychologist, "that you insist upon lying about your home situation?" The psychologist was sure that I had been lying about having to live in the barn and about being kicked out of school for playing a joke. "Well," I said, "I would like very much for you to come visit me at my house. You will see for yourself." She did not come to my house. Instead, she busied herself by writing symbols in her notebook while admonishing me about the horrors of telling lies.

Never once did she take any interest in what I told her. Instead, she seemed more interested in the fact that I could speak. However, once she asked me how I felt. This was new. Nobody had ever asked me how I felt before. Kids, I thought, were not supposed to have feelings. They were only supposed to obey.

6

Running Away Again

I ran away again. This time I was going to visit the psychologist at the hospital. I was going to visit her while wearing my smelly barn clothes. I was going to ask her to be like my new mother. She had been the only person who had ever asked me anything about how I felt, or what I wanted to be, for as long as I could remember, so maybe she really did care about me, even though she tried to make her interface very clinical and professional. Maybe she would let me stay at her house. I could go to high school in Worcester. I started to make plans. Surely, she would never send me back to my parents, especially once she learned that I wanted her to be like a mother to me. She would be so proud!

I started the long walk towards Worcester again. This time, I had no money. I was lucky and got a ride in a pickup truck almost the entire way to Paxton. Since I had arrived in Paxton somewhat refreshed by the ride, I hiked up the hill to the radio station overlooking the city of Worcester. This radio station was WTAG-FM. The *Worcester Telegram and Evening Gazette* owned it. I had always wanted to see the inside of a radio station. I was going to work at one some day. The engineer in attendance at the station showed me the giant FM radio transmitter complex. I explained to him that I was an amateur radio operator, but I had never seen the real thing before. I was overwhelmed by the immensity and complexity of the facility. Certainly, I just had to work there someday!

After the visit, I started back down the hill from the radio station. This time, I took a shortcut and walked down the side of the mountain through the woods. By the time I got to Worcester, I had been walking about ten miles cross-country through some very rough territory and I was quite tired. I was used to walking; I would think nothing about walking five or ten miles to visit somewhere secretly. However, I was frail, about six feet tall, but I weighed less than 120 pounds. I was so thin I could practically hide behind a hoe handle. I came to rest upon a Coke machine at a gas station on Chandler Street in Worcester. I would have to continue my journey to the hospital in the morning. I was so tired. I was also cold. There was snow on the ground. The police found me and called my parents. Now, I was in real bad trouble again.

7

The First Foster Home

The only time my father ever beat me in anger was that night. He used the buckle end of his belt and I was very hurt. I was injured and allowed to stay in the house while my parents were finding out what to do with me. Soon the word came! I was going to move to a foster home in Barre, Massachusetts. The place was called the Stetson Home for Boys. I was told it
was a nice place. The superintendent's name was Mr. Cutting. I met him and he seemed very nice. He told me that I would be attending Barre High School, and that everything was all set. I was expected in school next Monday.

The Stetson home was an institutional foster home, in which the residents lived like prison inmates. Each of us had our individual jobs to perform on the farm. The farm produced milk from dairy cows and had a truck garden that we would tend in warmer weather. This work farm used forced child labor to earn money. As an indentured servant, in return for my work, I was provided a place to stay, clothing, and some food. My first job at the farm was to get up at four o'clock in the morning to work in the barn. I was not allowed to use the milking machines yet. I was only allowed to clean the manure from the stalls. More responsibility would come later I was told. If indentured servitude of a child seems unbelievable, note that at the time in the state of Massachusetts, a child under eighteen years of age had no rights. Such children were the property of their parents, and could even be sold. In addition, child labor laws did not pertain to farm labor. While a child still could not be forced to perform illegal acts such as prostitution, forced work such as indentured servitude was legal.

·I was the second youngest boy at the home. Billy Smith was the youngest boy. This is not his true name. I wish I could use his true name, but I do not know where he went, or even if he is still alive. He was thirteen. I was fourteen.

I shared a room with an older boy with the last name of Fitzgerald. I never knew his first name. He was called "Fitzie" for short and it was rumored that he had fits, so the name fit him fine. I stayed in that room for only about two weeks. I hated Fitzie so much that I told Mr. Cutting that he had beaten me up. I had not really been beaten. It was much worse, but I could not let anybody know what had really happened.

The second rape

I was standing in my pajamas, ready for bed, looking out the window at the falling snow when Fitzie grabbed me around the mouth from behind and taped my mouth and hands with a roll of white surgical tape. Then he threw me on my bed and put his knee on my chest. I could not breathe. He told me that he was going to give me what I wanted and that if I made any sounds he would kill me. "If you don't give me any problems, I will let you go after I am through," he said, "or else, I will take your carcass out to the woods and hang you from a tree."

He removed my pajamas bottom. He removed all of his clothes. He was large. I had never seen anybody with an organ as huge as that! I was frightened, but strangely fascinated by it all, as though it were not really happening, just a wild nightmare. Then the pain began. He put my legs over his shoulders and then pressed at me so hard that I could no longer resist penetration. I had to "give in." I was being raped. Running nearly naked, I escaped to the boiler room, tearing off the tape as I ran. The pain lasted over two weeks. I bled so many times that I kept throwing away my undershorts until I healed. Until I got a new room, I slept on an old cot in the boiler room.

The boiler room was in a separate building that was a lot warmer than the barn. The attendant gave me a job in the boiler room. I was to get up at the usual time, 4:00 AM, and instead of going to the barn, I was to shovel a walk to the boiler room. After that, I was to use a heavy tool to shake the grates. Any clinker that remained was to be removed using a poker. Then the ashes were to be shoveled into a wheelbarrow and brought out to the ash pit. After this, I was to shovel in 19 to 20 shovels full of coal, then open the damper to start up the boiler. Some sight gauges showed the water level. If the water levels were low, I would open a valve to bring up the water level to a tape mark on the sight gauges.

This was to be done every morning. Eventually the attendant would come to work and he would sit in the boiler room and watch the boiler while reading magazines and filling out racing forms.

It was a very cold winter when I lived in Barre. The clothes that I wore were not too much help. All the boys at Stetson wore tennis shoes, sneakers as they were called back in those days. I had a navy blue felt coat, several sizes too large, with anchors embossed on the buttons. I had no mittens or gloves. In this outfit, I set out one Saturday afternoon for New Braintree, because I had learned that my parents had just moved there. My father had decided to become a minister. I thought that I could run away from Stetson and ask my parents to take me back. Surely, I thought, if I could only go back home everything would turn out all right. I'd ask my parents' forgiveness for everything I'd ever done wrong and I could start all over again and they would be proud of me the way they were so proud of my sisters. The distance from Barre to New Braintree was about eight miles.

I started the trip in high spirits. Off I went across the snowfields behind the Stetson farm. I was going to navigate through South Barre overland since it was very much shorter than taking the highway. I guessed that the distance was about five miles to South Barre. I had not anticipated the deep snowdrifts or the stream that I had to cross on the way. By the time I got to South Barre, it was very late in the afternoon and my feet were painfully frozen. My sweat had run out across my collar and had frozen around my neck. I was exhausted. When I got to the main highway in South Barre, I stood by the side of the road and hitchhiked back to Barre. The total trip had taken over six hours to travel only about four miles. There was no way I was going to be able to make it to New Braintree in the wintertime.

When I got back to Stetson, I had to go to bed without any supper because I had been missing without permission. I had missed both lunch and supper. For the next several weeks, I was very sick, but I continued to go to school anyway.

In school, I asked my new friend, Wendell Stanley, if I could borrow his bicycle some weekend soon. I told him that I was going to try to visit my folks. He said it would be okay, but told me that it is very hard to ride a bicycle when there is snow on the street. He had a fine three-speed bicycle, so I knew that he was a good friend since he would let me borrow his most valuable possession. I never did borrow his bicycle.

8

The Rocket

I met my friend Wendell while attending Barre High School. He and I had some common interests. He liked to make rockets and cannons out of gunpowder from his father's hand-loading equipment. One time we made a cannon that fired a large bolt entirely through a four-by-four. That gunpowder was powerful stuff. I got some zinc dust and sulfur from the high school laboratory and made some rockets. I used the black gunpowder as a primer to start the combustion. The igniter consisted of an exploding wire powered by a neon sign transformer. Some of my first rockets were crude, consisting of little more than a cardboard mailing tube and some zinc-sulfur fuel. Many just fizzled and spread burning sulfur around, setting small fires here and there.

As my techniques advanced, I finally made some of the rockets actually fly! They would climb straight up and I lost sight of several during my experiments. I had started to make them out of metal tubing, with real expansion nozzles and fins. My pride and joy was six feet tall! I fired it once and it took me over two weeks to find where it had fallen. I decided that the next time I fired it I was going to do it at dusk so I could follow the light in the sky. I was never much at mathematics, but I learned what I had to know so that, using a homemade protractor for sighting the elevation, I could find out how high the rocket flew. On its penultimate flight, it flew to a height of over three thousand feet!

Because of the space race after the Russians had achieved orbit of their Sputnik, there was a great deal of interest by high school students and their instructors in the science of rocketry. One of our class trips was to the Worcester Auditorium where General Electric demonstrated a very impressive and loud pulsejet engine. It was at this show that I started dreaming about making a really powerful rocket.

In high school, we studied, at least to our grade level, the mechanisms by which both rockets and jet engines worked.

There was an old carriage house at Stetson that had been used for storage. There was no lock on the door, so I found that if I moved some of the old wagon and boiler parts around, there was plenty of room for a workshop. I asked Mr. Cutting if I could use the carriage house for a workshop. He said, "Yes, but you'll have to clean it out first and bring all the junk to the dump." Bringing all the junk to the dump was nearly impossible because a lot of the stuff, such as old engines and boiler parts, was too heavy for anyone to lift. I chained a lot of stuff to the tractor and dragged it away. It was a lot of work, but now I had a workshop. Once the farm foreman learned that I had used the tractor, he was livid, but he did not have the authority to punish me. Instead, he noted that I knew how to drive the tractor, so if anybody got sick I could spread the manure.

You need to mix the fuel and oxidizer in a uniform manner to get uniform results. With my rocket, there was no oxidizer, but a reactant, sulfur. This had previously been prepared (by other experimenters) by melting the sulfur and mixing it with the zinc (very dangerous, as it could explode at any time). The molten paste would then be poured into the rocket casing and allowed to cool. My technique used plaster of paris! I would mix zinc, sulfur, and plaster of paris (about ten percent) while cool and dry. I would then add water to form a paste. This paste would be poured into the rocket casing and allowed to harden. I used a waxed wooden dowel running through the center of the rocket to form a burning chamber. After the fuel had hardened, I would remove the dowel. This left a nice uniform combustion space extending the entire length of the rocket. A small amount of black gunpowder was all that was needed to start the combustion and make the rocket fly. Many amateur rocketry experimenters used the melting method of pouring the fuel. Since I did not have any special equipment necessary to maintain precisely the temperature of the sulfur above its melting point, but below its burning point, I had to invent another method.

One of the things that this technique did was slow down the reaction of the sulfur and zinc. The result was a smooth steady combustion rather than an explosive reaction. I believed that there was no size or weight limitation to a rocket made in this manner. If you wanted the rocket to go higher, you simply made it larger, so that it could contain more fuel.

I had not learned about all the technical terms like "specific impulse," but I had a good concept about what was needed to make a rocket fly. One of my early concepts was only much later found in technical literature. Students were once taught that a rocket's thrust was created by an unbalance of forces. This was referred to as "Newton's principle." The idea was that if you had an enclosed pressure chamber that contained, say, 500 pounds per square inch of pressure, and you put a one-square-inch hole in one end, the resulting thrust would be 500 pounds because of the unbalanced pressure resulting from the one-square-inch hole.

I discovered that the shape of the hole made much more difference in the rocket's thrust than its size. I made many kinds of nozzles for my rocket using the lathe at school. The most successful nozzle seemed to be bell-shaped. Nowadays this is called a convergent-divergent design, and it is even used on the space shuttle.

I also found that the center of thrust was not, as described in the literature of the day, at the top of the rocket, but somewhere near the rear, close to the nozzle. This made these rockets seem top-heavy when under power, so it was mandatory to use some kind of stabilization to keep them flying straight. Since I did not have any electronic equipment onboard my rockets, I used very large fins for stabilization. These combinations of techniques made it possible to have a reusable rocket. All I had to change between flights was the nozzle. The nozzle would burn up as the flight progressed, since many were made of cold-rolled steel and even brass.

In order to get some more fuel, I hitchhiked back to North Brookfield, where I knew a former paper route customer who worked in the Quabaug Rubber factory. He gave me about fifteen pounds of sulfur. I could not find any more zinc dust, so I decided to use aluminum powder instead. I got this from the high-tech optical factory, Frank Cook Optics. For the igniter, I used black gunpowder from my friend Wendell.

Back in the carriage house beside the barn at Stetson, I carefully prepared my rocket. I did not know what proportion of aluminum powder to sulfur I should use. I did not even know if the resulting aluminum sulfide even existed, or would produce the specific impulse I needed without blowing up. I just assumed that aluminum was just a bit more "reactive" than zinc, so I should use less of it. I could not wait to fire the rocket, but I knew I had to wait for good weather when the winds were calm and the sun was setting so I could follow the glint of the rocket as it climbed into the air.

The third rape

During my short stay at Stetson, I had two other sexual experiences. I did not seek these things out. I just found out that at institutions where there are both small boys and larger, older, boys living in the same environment, these things happened all the time.

An older boy named Bob, who no longer attended school, but worked at the farm, confronted me one early evening and forced my mouth down over his penis. I gagged and vomited through my nose. He threatened to get Fitzie after me if I told anyone. I wanted to die. I felt for sure that my life was worthless from that time on. I had become a faggot. I had let someone violate my body in every way possible. I could not stand even thinking about myself. I needed to go somewhere else. Maybe I should try to run away again. I could not stay here. Fitzie had told others, so I was sure that I would be raped anytime anyone wanted. I was also confused. I could not possibly understand how anyone would ever do such things to anyone else. I had had erections before, but that was something private and secret. I could not imagine how anyone could have an erection while abusing someone. Erections and violence just did not go together, I reasoned. Furthermore, as a late bloomer, I did not even have a libido until I was about sixteen years of age so, truly, I did not have a clue.

In the era in which I was growing up, boys were expected to defend themselves to the death over things like rape. Since I had chickened out, it seemed that I no longer deserved to live.

Several weeks passed as I kept quietly busy modifying my rocket and doing some really interesting experiments in the physics laboratory at school. I made a mercury arc lamp that really worked. I was able to create plasma in an evacuated glass tube and ionize it with a homemade RF oscillator—hardly the thing to get me immediate entrance into Princeton University, but nonetheless something that I was able to create and understand all by myself. I had started to recover my self-esteem. Wendell was a good friend and helped with the experiments. The physics teacher was also very helpful and allowed me unlimited access to the lab.

9

The Night Visitor

One night after I had gone to bed a strange thing happened. Billy Smith opened the door of my room, walked over to my bed and climbed into my bed beside me. This thirteen-year-old was the youngest boy at Stetson.

He whispered in my ear, "Fuck me." I retorted, "What? What are you saying?" He said, "Please fuck me, pleeese..." I told him that I would never do that to anybody. I could not understand how he would actually want somebody to do something so horrible like that to him. I told him to go away.

He said he wanted to stay. In this bizarre way, he had shared a secret with me. Other boys had abused him many times. He felt that if the others thought he already had a boyfriend, they would leave him alone. This was all quite new to me. I never thought boys would have boyfriends. I told him, "Nobody will ever hurt you again. If anybody tries, find me. I will kill the fucker."

Now I shared with him my most private and precious secret. I told him about my rocket! Far into the night, we whispered about my rocket, how far it had flown, what it was made of, what it used for fuel. Nobody but Billy and Wendell ever knew about my rocket.

Billy slept in my bed that night. This was the first time I ever slept in the same bed with anyone else. Somehow, I felt a certain kind of warmth. I was protecting Billy from the evil that was lurking all about. I felt strong and important. I had a purpose. Just for tonight, Billy was safe. I would not let anybody touch him. He could sleep soundly with me at his side. Early in the morning, he left when I went to do my chores in the boiler room. I never saw Billy again.

10

The Second Fire

I was so confused and bothered about by night visitor that I cried in school the following day. All I could think about was Billy. I wanted to know where he was, how he was doing, if anybody was trying to hurt him again, what I could do to help him. Even my homeroom teacher noticed my eyes were red from crying. I told her I had gotten some

road salt into my eyes when I walked to school in the morning. She knew I was lying, but did not press me for any more answers.

Tonight, after school, I was going to fly my rocket! I could no longer wait for warmer weather and calm winds. This was the night I was going to make it climb five or six thousand feet into the air. It was going to go a mile high.

After I finished my farm chores, I set up the rocket behind the carriage house. I tried to find Billy. I was going to fly my rocket for him. I could not find him anywhere. I painted in red, white, and blue on the side of the rocket, "B SMITH X-1."

My method of setting off the igniter was crude. I simply ran an extension cord out the window and, at the appropriate time, I plugged it in. Then I would run outside and watch the rocket climb. I would record the elevation as many times as I could and try to keep it in sight as it fell. This time, it was different. There was a loud whoosh, then several popping sounds. I knew from the sound that it was not climbing away as it should. I looked out the window and it was gone. Out the door I ran, to scan the sky for it. It could not see it anywhere. I watched and waited. My beautiful rocket was gone! I could not find it anywhere. Not even a trail of smoke to follow. It was lost!

Then I saw smoke coming from the barn. I ran to the barn and smelled the odor of burning sulfur. I knew that the worst had happened. The entire hayloft was on fire. Then I ran to the house and yelled, "Fire!" I told everyone I saw that the barn was on fire then ran back to the barn and helped turn the animals loose. By now, just about everyone who worked on the farm was wrestling with the yokes to release the cows and send them out towards the pasture. Soon the smoke was too hot and heavy, so we all retreated towards the safety of the main building. The barn burned to the ground, and with it, my rocket and my dreams. As I watched the milk cooler compressor explode, my insides seemed to explode with it. No cattle were lost, but a barnyard cat was lost and presumably died in the fire.

11

The Inquisition and Trial

About ten o'clock that night, Mr. Cutting asked what I knew about the fire. I told him that I started it! I started crying and told him about the rapes. I did not tell him about the rocket since I did not want anyone to find it and see Billy's name on it. I was going to go this one alone. Mr. Cutting was not interested in the rapes. The State Police Fire Marshal investigated and interrogated me until about four o'clock in the morning. I really cannot remember what I told him. I would have told him anything he wanted. I was rushed off to a court holding cell in Worcester.

There is not much to say about the trial. I remember the marble columns in front of the courthouse, the long blue-white granite steps leading to the copper doorway covered with green patina, and the sound of interior doors as they were locking behind me. I wondered how many had passed this way—what had happened to them, where they had gone. The court holding cell contained a toilet without a seat in the center of the floor. The walls displayed the names of many who had been locked within. I read many names and saw the dates left by those before me to mark their passing along this way. I did not have a pencil to mark my name. I was afraid that nobody would ever know I had come this way, perhaps to disappear forever. Mostly, I was afraid of being alone.

In Massachusetts, in 1959, the judge of the Juvenile Court was the judge, the jury, and the law. I did not have an attorney. In fact, I was not allowed to have an attorney, even if I could have afforded it. As a juvenile, I was not entitled to a trial by jury. In fact, I was not even entitled to a trial. The Juvenile Court tribunal was

35

called a hearing to get around all the Constitutional mumbo jumbo. I was not offered any defense. I was not even asked if I was guilty! The judge simply stated in a monotone voice, "The charge is arson, to which I find you guilty. You are hereby remanded to the custody of the Youth Service Board. See if they can find what to do with you. Take him away. Next..."

In spite of the fact that the judge had said I was guilty, in principle he had merely found me a delinquent child, not guilty or innocent, because he was not allowed to make that determination. Judges talk with forked tongues. The determination of guilt or innocence was to be made by the Youth Service Board.

12

The Detention Center

The Massachusetts Youth Service Board Reception and Detention Center was in Roslindale, Massachusetts, on 450 Canterbury Street, across an iron fence from the Forest Hills Cemetery. I will remember that address for the rest of my life. This place became known as the "Center." There was a board, the Youth Service Board, consisting of three people.  One of them, Mr. Turley, was a very rotund man. One of the other members was a woman with long green fingernails. Their purpose, so I understood, was to decide into what institution the unfortunate arrivals were to be placed. They made their own rules.

Massachusetts had several reform schools from which to choose. The Lyman School in Westborough was the oldest and most famous. There was the Shirley School, Bridgewater State Reformatory, some nuthouse in Mattapan, a girl's reformatory in Lancaster, and several others of lesser importance. Gallows humor had everyone going to Lancaster.

The building was a brick and concrete structure of wide expanse. It had three floors, a cafeteria, a gymnasium, and an outdoor fenced-in basketball court. It looked like a really nice place. The corridors were lined with heavy wooden doors, each the entrance to a small private room. There were no bars on the windows or the doors. The facility was nearly brand new, and music played from the loudspeakers hidden in the ceiling tiles over the corridors. The music was from radio station WCOP in Boston. It played day and night. I was soon to learn that a nice building does not make a nice place to stay.

An officer of the court had transported me alone to the facility. He had brought his wife along for the ride. The court officer told me not to worry; that he had brought many boys to the Center and it was a really good place. I would even have my own room and go to the Center's private school while I was waiting to see the Board. "They'll probably just send you home after they do their tests," I was told. "It's not like the reformatory. That's where they take the real bad guys," the officer continued.

My court hearing had been in Worcester. About twenty miles from Worcester, on the way to the Center, was the Lyman School for Boys in Westborough. As we passed by on State Route 9, the officer pointed it out: "Now that's where they send the real bad boys. Lyman School and Shirley School, that's where they go." When I first saw Lyman School, I was overwhelmed with fear. I could not imagine having to stay at a place like that.

When we arrived at the Center, I was led inside through two steel doors to the induction area. After the officer left, I was told to strip. I removed all my clothes except my underpants. The guard, who I now quickly learned was to be called a "Master," and addressed as "Sir," yelled, "I told you to remove *all* your fucking clothes." I removed my underpants. I will not go into all the details, but the Master proceeded to remark about how I hardly had any genitals at all, that I was not going to survive a week, and that my only hope was to be real nice to the Masters or "you'll find your little ass in a sling."

My wallet and clothes were put into a brown paper sack and marked with a seven-digit number, 2093603. I was given a pair of brown pants several sizes too large, a maroon polo shirt, and a pair of white stockings. Since I was not allowed to have a belt, I learned quickly how to do everything with one hand since the other was always used to hold up my pants. After the induction, it was late in the evening, so I was escorted to my room. Five boys inhabited the room, just the right size for one small person. I was now number six!

The room had two small iron beds set in the concrete floor. An angle-iron rail ran around each bed to hold a mattress. There were no mattresses. Each boy had a thin blanket and used part of it to cover the railing on the bed, so he could sit half prone without too much pain from the iron ridge. One boy was lying on the floor. He was literally covered with dried blood. No one spoke, or made any sound the entire night. This room was very cold. I was cold during my entire stay at the Center.

I awoke early and watched the snow piling up on the windowsill. An iron window opened about four inches. As a youngster, I knew that if I could get my head through an opening, I could get the rest of my body through it also. Even though it was very cold, I opened the window to see just how far it would go. I knew right away that I would never be able to crawl through that exit. With the window closed, I stepped over the other boys and went back to my perch on the edge of the bed. When the morning came, the Masters unlocked the doors and ordered everyone out of the rooms.

First, there were the showers, rapidly executed with a Master holding a cold-water garden hose on those that hesitated too long under the dribble of water from the showerheads; then breakfast at the cafeteria. Breakfast consisted of oatmeal with no sugar, and a glass of powdered milk. Incidentally, this was the menu every day except Sunday, when we had powdered eggs and lukewarm tea. Lunch was macaroni, sometimes with cheese, and supper was toast with dried beef. This menu repeated every day!

After breakfast, we would go to the dayroom where those who had their parents' permission would be given one cigarette to smoke. I thought it strange that, in order for you to be a resident here, you must have disobeyed your parents, but once here you needed your parents' permission to smoke. I did not smoke, so I did not care. The dayroom contained a television set that was partially obscured inside an iron cage. I had not seen much TV, so it was a new experience for me. I enjoyed just about everything that I saw on the television.

I spent a lot of time trying to figure out how it worked. I could understand how the picture was made up of many lines with dark and light patches, which, if you stood back, would blend into a picture, but I wanted to find out how the television station knew when to change the lines to dark and light when there were so many television sets tuned in. I had been told that the television stations must pick up signals from the television sets that told it where the lines were all the time.

Television stations must be very complex, I thought, to be able to do all that. I wondered just how many television sets could be tuned in before the station would lose track and get all messed up. In the three months that I stayed at the Center, I invented in my mind a way of keeping all the television sets synchronized with the transmitter, so the transmitter didn't have to do all the work. The invention would allow an unlimited amount of television sets to be tuned in. This meant that everyone could own a television set and there would still be enough picture to go around.

I truly did not know that the invention was, in fact, what was being used presently. I envisioned a few details differently, but that invention itself had preceded me by about twenty years. I had reinvented television because somebody had given me the wrong information about how television worked.

Keeping my mind occupied by these things, like the technical nature of television, was the method that I used to survive at the Center. I was to learn much more about man's cruelty to man at the Center than any fourteen-year-old boy ought to know.

I watched the Masters beat many boys at the Center. This happened so often (several times a day) that I soon got used to it. I learned to stay behind somebody else, out of the direct line of sight of a Master, to minimize my chances of being hurt or abused. Sometimes a Master would pull a boy from a line and slam him against the wall or punch him in the stomach. The boy's offense might only have been that he did not stand up straight or that he was not looking straight ahead. The worst offense was when a boy did not say, "Yes, *sir*" when addressed.

I will always remember the first time I saw a boy beaten by a Master. The Master looked at a boy and said, "You, punk, what's your name?" The boy meekly responded with his name. "What? Punk, you don't have a name," the Master yelled. "You're a bastard, you don't have a name, your mother's a whore! She fucks all the sailors. Isn't that right?" "No!" said the boy. "No, what?" demanded the Master as he grabbed the boy by the hair with his left hand. "No sir!" yelled the boy as he put both hands to his head in pain. "Yes, *sir*," said the Master, "you're just a bastard of a cocksucking whore, right?" "No, *sir!*" responded the boy. "You fucking bastard, how *dare* you yell at me!" demanded the Master as he threw a right uppercut to the boy's stomach that seemed to lift him off his feet. The boy then curled up on the floor as the Master walked over to another boy and did much the same.

Most all of the beatings worked this way. The Master would first insult the boy's parentage and provoke him to talk back, at which time words were replaced by fists. Most boys had been beaten before they arrived at the Center. You could tell if one had just been sent up from Dorchester. Boys from Dorchester, it seemed, always arrived beaten up. The boy on the floor of my room the first night at the Center had come from Dorchester.

If you sat in a group with some other boys, the Masters would sometimes start kicking the boys apart if they felt that there were too many in the same area. There were no chairs in the dayroom, so we would sit on the floor or stand against the wall. I was never beaten at the Center. I guess I was too small and skinny to be much sport. The Masters had other plans for me.

A few more rapes

I had been moved into a room that I shared with only two other boys. These beds had mattresses and one of the boys slept on a mattress on the floor. Since there were no springs on the beds, it did not matter much whether one slept on the floor or on a bed. The lights were always left on until 10:00 PM, at which time the doors were unlocked for access to the toilet, and the lights were turned off. A bright light showed through the door's window, so it was never dark in the rooms.

One night after lights out, I heard a scream. It was a horrible scream followed by silence. A few minutes later, I heard some continuous sobbing that became louder as one of the Masters dragged a boy back to his room. The boy on the floor said, "They got another one!" I asked him what he meant. "Did the boy try to run away and get caught?" I asked. "You'll find out soon enough!" was his reply.

Two nights later, I found out. After lights out, a Master came to my room and lifted me out of bed. He was about six feet tall, had red hair and a scar on his right cheek. His ears were very tiny compared to the rest of his head. I would guess that he was about thirty years old. I would find out soon enough that he had reddish brown hair all over his body, including his back. He put a finger to my lips and told me not to be afraid. He said, "We are just going to have a little fun." He carried me out to the dayroom and raped me on the floor in front of the television. I did not scream. I just watched the television. The Master was not very gentle, and he did not use any lubricant. I was bleeding when he was through. He told me not to worry: "The bleeding will go away."

When I got back to my room, the boy on the floor asked me how I liked the party. I told him that it was not too bad since he did not tie me up. He called me a faggot and went to sleep.

Although I was still bleeding, I was raped again the following two nights. By now, I was so used to this abuse that I even joked, "Well let's get this over with so I can get back to bed!" I would not kiss the Master and I even bit his lip the last night with him. Perhaps that is why he left me alone after the third night.

The bleeding did not go away. By the end of the third week, I was very sick and could no longer walk. I had to crawl to the dayroom and the cafeteria with the Masters taunting me all the way. I could no longer sleep on the floor of the dayroom, near the wall where the warm steam pipes went on their way to the cafeteria. I sometimes just sat in the corner staring at the television that I could no longer see. Eventually some kindhearted Master reported that I was sick and I was brought to the infirmary. I had a high fever and began treatment with antibiotics and suppositories. The nurse reported that I had a slight case of pneumonia. "Probably something that you brought here with you," she announced in a matter-of-fact way. I spent over three months waiting for the promised Board interview. Over one month was spent in the infirmary.

On Sunday there were visiting hours. My parents came to see me every Sunday. They brought me candy bars and some electronics books and magazines. My parents lived over sixty miles from the Center at Roslindale. I always loved them even during the hardest times. I never told them so. My parents also visited me in the infirmary. I told them that I was getting better. I never told them anything else.

Visiting parents were never allowed into the facility where the boys actually lived. Instead, a friendly receptionist who worked only on Sunday greeted them. They were then led into a nice room with a long oaken table and many chairs, and then greeted by their child as he was brought into the room by a uniformed, clean-cut, professional-looking guard. This was a charade.

After I recovered from my bout with pneumonia, I started to talk with other boys at the Center. Often we would be escorted to the gym and we would sit along the walls to talk and play cards. There was no gym equipment, no basketballs, or anything like that. The gym was used as another dayroom while the main one was being cleaned, or when, as in several cases, it was too crowded. I met several boys my age who had an interest in electronics. I also met one who had made a rocket, but he had not been sent up for arson. He was a stubborn child. His stepfather had put him here. A Master had also raped him. We became friends because we had a common enemy.

"So how do they get away with this shit?" I asked my new friend.

He said, "So, you tell me—would you tell your mother?"

"No way. She'd say I was either weak, or a lying bastard. Once she thought I sold my body to get a shortwave radio," I said.

"How about your old man?" was his next query.

"No way, I'd get killed." I responded.

"How about the police?" was another query.

"You're outta your mind! They'd laugh and probably beat me up," I responded.

"Yep," he said, "about the only thing you could do is, maybe tell a priest. Even that...hell, a lot of priests are 'funny' themselves; they'd say you should just say some Hail Mary's and you'll be okay." He continued, "So somebody finds out that perverts can work here. Perverts have got pervert friends. Soon as there is an opening, their friend gets the job. Pretty soon, the whole place's filled with perverts. That's how it happens. It's just like the cops. If you get your rocks off by beating up kids, you go to work as a cop. Same thing. There's no way it'll ever change because the cops always protect the cops." After a moment he concluded, "Like nobody who wasn't a *preevert* would wanta work here."

I talked to another boy who had been sent up twice. They did not touch him the first time, but they got him the second night he was at the Center on his second trip.

He said to me, "You can't tell who they will take, but they always go in twos! It's as if they wait until there's a pair of them that has an eye on a pair of boys. That's when it happens." I did not tell him that I was alone when it happened to me.

Regardless of how it came about, there appeared to be an underlying principle of abuse at the Center. This principle was to make physical and sexual abuse so egregious that any such reported events would be unbelievable. Children sent to the Center were considered *de facto* liars anyway, so as long as the abuse was extreme, the Masters who perpetrated this abuse were unlikely to be caught and punished. As a child, I was careful not to tell anybody about this abuse, because I did not want to be thought of as a liar, or worse, if anyone believed me, somebody who did not defend his sexuality to the death, if necessary.

In 1646 the General Court of Massachusetts Bay Colony had enacted a law where "a stubborn or rebellious son, of sufficient years and understanding," would be brought before the magistrates in court and "such a son shall be put to death." Stubborn child laws were also enacted in Connecticut, Rhode Island, and New Hampshire.

Of course, such stubborn children were not put to death in the fifties…or were they? Mark Devlin's account in his book, *Stubborn Child*, illustrates a slow death. At the age of fifty-six, Mark died, having been killed by the State of Massachusetts Juvenile Court System. As a small child, he spent time at the YSB Detention Center and Lyman School. His crime was that he kept slightly out of reach of his alcoholic father, so he would not be beaten anymore.

Most of the inmates were at the Center for crimes like truancy, being a stubborn child, getting kicked out of school (delinquency), and statutory rape, which means the girl told her mother after she had sex with her boyfriend. I met a real criminal, too. He had killed his brother over a five-dollar bottle of whiskey. He had a nice sense of humor, and was a very likable person.

Largely the most common crime was breaking and entering (or B & E, as we called it). This was a catchall crime that was usually associated with stubborn child cases and delinquency. Often, when a child was running away from the police, he would enter an old building and hide. This produced the contrived rationale for the B & E charge.

In Massachusetts, breaking into an abandoned building was a misdemeanor if done during the daylight hours, but suddenly became a felony in the nighttime. Many old cities like Boston have many abandoned buildings. They sometimes were neat places for boys to play, unless, of course, the police caught them. If this happened, they would be beaten up by the police and then sent to the YSB.

Another crime was grand theft. This was the charge when some boys would go joyriding in an automobile that did not belong to them. In many cases, the boys would drive around in the automobile until the police caught them, or until they ran out of gas. Almost never damaged, the car was usually returned to its owner by the police. Perhaps there should have been a civil suit against the boys for inconveniencing the car owner, or using ten dollars worth of gasoline without permission, but grand theft seemed to me to be a rather excessive charge. In any event, car owners would continually leave their ignition keys in their cars, enticing teenagers into jail.

The police also used the Youth Service Board Detention Center as a place to keep youngsters that they had abused (beat up) incommunicado, so the police would not have to answer for their crimes. I already told you about Dorchester. Everybody I ever met from Dorchester had been beaten up by the police. Some boys had not been sent to this Detention Center by the courts. They were simply driven there by the police and left for a few weeks to soften them up.

Of course, there were boys at the YSB who had been involved in actual heavy crimes like robbery and murder. However, these were not like the delinquents stereotyped in movies and magazines. You know what I mean, the ones with the switchblades who kill for kicks. I never met any inmate either at the YSB or at Lyman School who was anything like the stereotypical delinquent. Instead, it was the Masters at the YSB who were like the stereotypical delinquents, only older, and much crueler. The two kids I met who had killed somebody, killed for a damn good reason (so they thought). One killed his stepfather after he had beat up his mother. The other accidentally killed his brother when they were both drunk and fighting over the last bit of whiskey in a bottle.

If either of these kids had had proper representation in a real court of law, neither would have been sent up for any crimes. In the case of the kid killing his brother, it was obviously an accident brought about by excessive alcohol consumption. A jury certainly would have exonerated the one who killed his stepfather. The problem was that in Massachusetts, juveniles were not entitled to trials, much less juries.

Research about my incarceration at the YSB has revealed that the Massachusetts 1948 Youth Service Act was never fully implemented. One of the implemented parts of this act removed so-called juvenile offenders from the control of the courts as far as direct verdicts and sentencing were concerned. Adjudication of guilt or as a delinquent child resulted in the youth being sentenced, as a juvenile delinquent, to the Youth Service Board for an undetermined sentence for evaluation, treatment, and incarceration, if necessary.

Since courts were no longer allowed to use their own wisdom in trying juvenile offenders, many judges took a very punitive approach to even potential offenders by denying them even the chance to speak in their courtrooms. This was a misguided attempt to fight the corrupt system by punishing its victims.

Contrary to its name, the Department of Youth Services did not have anything to do with service to youth. Like many distorted institutional names, the word "service" was a public relations invention. Such distortion is all too commonplace. For instance, many institutional names have the word "science" in them, like Christian Science, mortuary science, etc. They have nothing to do with science at all.

In addition to its failure to follow the laws of the State regarding prompt evaluation and processing of detainees, the Youth Service Board used its authority to provide temporary foster homes to create a detention center that was second in horror only to certain World War II concentration camps.

Eventually this detention center was discovered to be the den of iniquity that it was, and some reforms were accomplished. I'm told that it is no longer a place of child rape, but I am also told, by a person who works there, that he is not allowed to discuss anything that goes on inside. This does not give me a warm fuzzy feeling. Nevertheless, the YSB Detention Center was renamed the Judge Connolly Center in honor of the person who tried to change it.

13

I See the Board

The way it was supposed to work is that juvenile offenders would only spend a few days at the Center to undergo some evaluations and tests. One of the evaluations was supposed to be whether the detainee had actually done something wrong. After the tests were completed, the Youth Service Board would meet and, considering the results of these tests, determine to which facility, if any,  the youth would be sent. This should have taken just a few days.

In fact, there were no tests. There were no evaluations, just the warehousing of the boys until the larger institutions were able to accommodate their admission. Since many institutions were above capacity, detainees would simply wait until there was an opening at a target institution such as Lyman School. The selection of these target institutions seemed to be made entirely according to the age of the offender.

There was never any consideration given as to whether or not the detainee had actually committed an offense! The courts were not allowed to conduct trials, and the Youth Service Board failed to perform its function as specified by law. Let me make this *perfectly* clear. Children did not have *any* rights in the state of Massachusetts. There were no trials provided for juveniles because the 1948 Youth Service Act was never fully implemented.

The Board met each Wednesday. Finally, my Wednesday came and went. "Next week," I was told. Two weeks later, I did get to see the Board. I was shown into a room where three persons sat at a long table. The room was somewhat different because the windows were like household windows and did not contain the industrial-strength glass with its embedded chicken wire like the others. The bright outside light shone into a window, making the rest of the room comparatively dark, so it seemed as though I was seeing the light at the end of a tunnel. The man at the head of the table, Mr. Turley, introduced himself by extending a hand that was as large as a ham. He asked me to be seated. In his other hand there was a manila folder containing a single sheet of paper. He looked at the paper and frowned. "Reviewing the specifications, we hereby sentence you to the Lyman School for Boys in Westborough, Massachusetts, until such time as you have earned 700 credits. Any questions?" I shook my head no. "Dismissed," was his reply.

It turns out that the Youth Service Board usually prescribed 700 credits when sending boys to Lyman School. I never met any boy at Lyman School who had actually been interviewed by the Board. They simply waited until there was an opening and sent the next boy to fill that opening, after going through the motions as I described. The credit value served as a throttle. Since there were a fixed number of beds available in the available institutions, this throttle value was used to keep the Lyman School at a manageable overcapacity.

By the way, the number that I so carefully remembered, the one that was written on the sack that contained my belongings, 2093603, meant nothing. My clothes were returned to me, but not my wallet, when I was being prepared for the ride to the Lyman School. My wallet did not contain any money but it did contain everything left in the world that had belonged to me. Now I felt that as the final insult.

REFLECTIONS

The Last Elm Tree

Tall trees lean towards dark bricks, listening for the cries of lost souls trapped behind. Outside, the cemetery in silence waits. Many had passed this place on their way to hell. Hell was cold. Icy fingers holding the knife of fate attack from a silent mist, heavy and dark. This evil place on Canterbury Street was the very entrance to hell.

A small child is led inside, his hands bound by chains of hate. The trees whisper, "Was not this child, only yesterday, the one who played beneath our boughs, with singing songs and dances in the wind?"

An elder elm responds, "This child was damned from the start. I myself saw it in his eyes as soon as he came to play."

An ash tree stands. Pressing an ear to the earth, this young tree listens in search of truth. He shall know about these children and someday tell a troubled traveler who walks along the way.

A child lives with silent screams of anguish. The child dies. Raped of his childhood, only a naked shell remains. Cold shivers of hate crawl across his bloody back, his body twisting, tearing, torturing...

As the trees record the passing time, the young ash tree listens and hears each child's cries.

Another child arrives, then another, and another. The scene repeats. The elder elm implores, "These children were dead before they came. Waste not your time to hear these things. The law determines life. They broke the law, and so they die."

From darkened windows come muffled screams, loud voices filled with hate, soft cries, whispers, silence. A child's voice pleads in desperate prayer. The sky fills with angry clouds. The storm begins. Winds pound the walls with violent cascades of blackened snow. Those walls prevail. Defeated, the storm subsides. Gray skies remain.

Broken bodies, bent not with age, but burden, are shipped from here to places far away. These bodies, looking like small children, but bearing a weight so heavy no child could endure, bear witness to these changes made in hell.

One such child passes through these gates and disappears for forty years. This child was I. Returning like a moth drawn to the fire, I walk along this way seeking the wisdom of the trees that overlook this place. They line the wall. On one side in the cemetery are resting bodies; on the other are captured souls.

I inquire of the trees, "What has happened at this place since I have gone?" There is no response, only the soft murmur of the breeze whispering through the leaves.

I cry out, "Somebody must have seen these things! Somebody must have known! Did I come all this way to have never left a mark?"

Silence waits.

I walk to the foot of a tall ash tree, pause, and lean against its breast. The tree responds, "I remember you from so very long ago. You were crying when they took you here. You were so very small and frail. I remember your cries in the night. I even tried to comfort you with the music of my leaves when you called out in the night." I embrace the tree. I have found a long lost friend.

"Tell me," I ask, "what has happened to the others? Have they fared as well as me? Have they grown so tall and strong? Are they free?"

"No child who passed this way is ever free again. Many have borne their burdens well. But others have not." The tree quietly whispers, "Where I stand marks the very gates of hell. Some survive the passing, others fail."

I look out across the road and see the rotting trunk of a massive old elm tree hacked with chainsaws. Like bleached bones lying in the sun, this carcass remains. I ask the ash, "Was not this the stately elm that once stood guard along the way?"

"Yes," said the ash, "but he had a disease, so the authorities cut him down and killed him. It was the law, you know."

14

The Lyman School for Boys

The school looked like a college campus. It covered about a thousand acres near the top of Powder Hill off State Route 9 in Westborough. On the top of the hill stood a tall water tower that could be seen for many miles. To its right was Lyman Hall, the school's induction center. New inmates always stayed there first. Returnees—parole violators—went directly to Oak Cottage, the discipline cottage. Theodore Lyman, who was its principal benefactor before the turn of the century, founded the school. Boys lived in individual cottages, each capable of supporting about one hundred boys.

Lyman Hall and Chauncey

This reform school was founded in 1848 and was the oldest such institution in the country. Early on, it served just as a children's prison for boys who were too young to survive at men's prisons like Walpole. By the turn of the century, there began to be an emphasis upon behavioral modification, that is, reforming delinquent boys. In the late fifties, when I entered the school, there had been a lot of work done towards standardizing the inmates' treatment and, in general, improving his life. Some of the reformers were Mr. Borys, the school superintendent, and Mr. Kenney, his assistant. These men were determined not only to improve existing conditions, but also to make sure that a boy's stay at Lyman could serve a truly useful purpose, not only to society, but also to the boy himself.

The word cottage should not be confused with the idea of a little house by the side of the road. Each cottage was a three-story high, monstrous brick building of Federal and Queen Anne architecture containing an enormous dormitory on its top floor, a living area, which at one time had facilities for serving meals, and a basement area where lockers and wooden benches lined the walls. Most of the inmates' time would be spent in the basement area. The cottages where I stayed were Lyman Hall, Worcester, Oak, and Elms. There were at least six other cottages on the grounds.

The Lyman School had a farm with a large truck garden, a print shop, and a carpentry shop. It also had a recreation center that contained an auditorium, used as a movie theater and a church, a roller-skating rink, a gymnasium, and an indoor swimming pool. A power station contained a laundry shop, and additional buildings comprised an infirmary and the AB administration building. At the center of the grounds stood a new cafeteria, and a new school building, with grades only to the tenth. These buildings faced a softball field. This looked like a really nice place and, with few exceptions, it was!

There were no fences anywhere. In fact, the cottage doors were not locked, nor was there any way to lock them. Anybody who ran away would be disciplined in a manner that served to prevent runaways. This eliminated the requirements for locks. There were locks on some buildings such as the movie theatre, various trade shops, and the storage warehouse, but the living quarters were not locked. This openness was important and, in fact, traditional.

A Cottage Master and, usually, a Matron ran each of the cottages. Usually this husband-and-wife team lived on campus. The administration building was a small, neat wooden structure near the entrance to the facility. The two most important persons in that building were Mr. Borys and Mr. Kenney.

There was a full-time priest to minister to the needs of Catholic boys and a full-time Protestant minister also. The Protestant minister and counselor was a young man, Reverend F. Robert Brown. "Bob" Brown wanted to be called Bob (even though his first name was really Fred). He was to become one of the most important people in my young life. The Catholic priest was Father Fallon.

The first month

When I first came to Lyman, I was to stay at Lyman Hall. This cottage, which really consists of two cottages, is shown at the beginning of this chapter. The section on the left is Lyman Hall Cottage, and the section on the right is Chauncey Cottage. The Cottage Master at Lyman Hall was Mr. Stearns. Moreover, stern he was. Everything had to be just right. There was no talking while in line, no doing this or that. The rules were strictly enforced. I got my first "dollars" under Mr. Stearn's firm hand. The dollars were several slaps on the palm of the hand with a wooden board. The number of slaps depended upon the severity of the infraction. I was caught talking when I was not supposed to, so since it was my first offense, I only received two dollars. I never received another dollar during my entire stay at the school. I swear I can still feel those swollen fingers today!

The protocol at Lyman was designed so that there was positive reinforcement at all times. There were unvarying rules that were in place, sometimes for no good reason at all. The fact that the rules existed was sufficient for their required enforcement. Any person who broke one of these rules was severely punished. The punishment was always physical. In this way, the punishment was supposed to affect each person in precisely the same manner.

This approach was probably quite correct since, for example, if someone were quite accustomed to being yelled at, punishment by yelling would not affect that person the same as some timid person who had never experienced an unkind word. Of course, this is just an example. Only parents try to punish by yelling. Although severe physical punishment was used, I learned right away that it was fair. I never saw any boys punished for something that they had not done. The facts were that if you followed the rules precisely, nobody would ever punish you. That was something that you could count on. Furthermore, the punishment was always a measured response to the severity of the offense.

The usual punishment for rule infractions involved kneeling in an erect manner, so that one's weight was borne by the knees. The skin covering a boy's kneecaps was thin enough, so this would become painful within a few minutes. Some boys thought that the initial pain would get worse, and so became convinced that the punishment was horrific torture. This would lead to them crying or sitting down on their legs. This would sometimes result in the Master punishing the whole group.

The punishment of a group of boys for the infractions of an individual did not seem fair and probably was not. However, it did result in some mentoring whereby group pressure was brought to bear upon individuals who were not adjusting properly. Anyway, the group would convince the offender that the punishment was bearable by demonstrating that the pain was not only minimal, but would lessen as time went by. In this manner, the group became responsible for the behavior of every individual in that group. Although peer pressure in future life should not result in punishment, this did teach one to respect not only the persons in charge, but also one's peers.

Older or wiser peers provided additional mentoring, so that new residents could learn the ropes, as in the following example.

After residents had done their time as prescribed by the Youth Service Board, and were awaiting parole, they might be promoted to houseboy. When I was a

Lyman Hall houseboy during my second stay at the Lyman School, a new resident arrived who was very combative and attempted to fight Mr. Stearns. Although Mr. Stearns was middle-aged, he was a very smart fighter and promptly incapacitated his assailant by hitting him in the throat. When his assailant was down on his hands and knees trying to catch his breath, Mr. Stearns told two of us houseboys to teach him the ropes. He then went upstairs, probably to his apartment. His absence helped reinforce the notion that order would be maintained even if he were not always present.

What we did next was to help the boy to his place on the bench in front of his locker. Then we told him the rules from the perspective of somebody who had already been through the school and was awaiting parole. We told him how the credit system worked and that, if he behaved, he would earn 125 credits per month (but only 100 for the first month), that we were all in this together and that we would all help each other. I asked him how many credits he needed to earn. He told me, with a painful, quivering, barely audible voice, 700 (I guess this was a standard number meted out by the YSB). I told him that this was the same as I had to earn when I first came to Lyman. I could tell that he was combative because he was very scared, so I told him that when I first arrived at Lyman, I was so frightened that I could barely look anybody in the eye. I was ready to try to kill the first person who approached me.

"Now," I said, "look at me! I can do anything I want. I'm even going to outside school in Westborough! You can do this," I continued, "you just need to follow the rules." Actually, when I first arrived at Lyman I was so frightened that I would cry if anybody looked towards me. The little white lie seemed appropriate in these circumstances, and in fact was.

The other houseboy told him that Mr. Stearns was a very good man and that he was very fair. He convinced the assailant to apologize for trying to pick a fight. "Maybe," he said, "you won't get any demerits for the fight if you apologize."

When Mr. Stearns came back down the stairs, the assailant stood up, walked over to the Master's desk, and said with a recovering, but still quivering voice, "I'm sorry!" Mr. Stearns said, "Yes. I know. Sit down." There were no further events, or repercussions because of that fight.

Additional punishment, usually reserved for group punishment when the entire house had been slow in performing required tasks, or otherwise was in need of some attitude adjustment, involved shining floors on one's hands and knees with a shine brush. At Lyman Hall, the upstairs dayroom was always kept in immaculate condition in this manner because there was usually some need to adjust the attitude of newcomers. Remember that boys were usually assigned to other cottages after about a month in Lyman Hall. This meant that they were not usually subjected to such group punishment for very long because they were usually quite well-adjusted by the time they moved to another cottage.

Serious infractions of the no-talking-in-the-shower-room rule sometimes resulted in the talker having to clean a hopper (toilet) with a toothbrush. No, he did not have to use his personal toothbrush. I remember one boy having to clean the shower room floor with a toothbrush. It was probably the last time that he ever talked in the shower room. Even now, I do not sing in the shower!

The Masters took time to know each boy's name and to remember any slight infractions that they had let slide. This also meant that a boy would have a chance to redeem himself before having to undergo punishment. Once punishment was done; it was done. The boy had cleaned the slate, so to speak, by completing the punishment. This, I think, was important reinforcement of the idea that once you had paid for your infractions, you were complete and clean. This kind of reinforcement could help remove any guilt that an offender might otherwise retain when he was paroled back into society.

Regardless of whether the training methods used were correct, everyone in a position of authority at Lyman at the time thought that they were correct and tried their best to implement these methods in a fair and consistent manner. I never saw any individual singled out for unfair or unequal punishment while being supervised by the House Masters or Matrons. With one exception, I never saw anybody beat up at Lyman as I had seen at the Youth Service Center.

The rules were simple and precise:

Lyman School Rules

- No pushing or shoving.
- No talking while in line.
- No talking in the shower room.
- No talking in the dormitory.
- No talking in the cafeteria.
- No smoking except as supervised.
- No swearing.
- No fighting or aggressive behavior.
- No lying.
- No cheating at games.
- No hesitation at work.
- No running away.
- No money or private cigarettes allowed. Not applicable to houseboys.
- You must answer a Master with "Sir."
- You must answer a Matron with "Madam."
- You must do what a Master or Matron says.
- You must eat everything on your plate.
- You must answer any questions directly and truthfully.
- You must accept punishment without resistance.
- Queue up in line according to height.
- Shoes are to be kept shined.
- Lockers are to be kept clean and well-ordered.
- In the dormitory, beds are to be made with "hospital" corners in perfect order.
- On work detail, you continue working continuously until told to stop.

There may be a few other rules that I have long ago forgotten. The rules were never changed or suddenly recreated, so you did not have any unpleasant surprises.

Many of the boys at Lyman were street-smart, that is, they had learned the customs of the street, such as "Thou shalt not rat upon thy neighbor." They were not required to compromise those principles, but you were never allowed to lie. Let me give you an example.

Several months after I had arrived at Lyman, one of my friends had run away. Usually, runaways are picked up almost immediately by the State Police and returned within the first few hours. In this case, the boy disappeared while on work detail and he was not found quickly. During the boy's second day of absence, I was taken aside by the Cottage Master and asked if I knew where he might have gone. It was well-known that I had become a good friend of the runaway, so it was quite possible that I knew even his exact location. I told the Cottage Master that "I should never violate a confidence. Please don't ask me to violate that confidence. Please try to find another way to locate him. I will help you if I must, but I beg you to try to find another way!"

Now, these were very smart words from a fourteen-year-old kid, and the Cottage Master knew it. The Cottage Master, himself a very wise man, Mr. McCabe, hesitated for a moment, then said, "OK...talk to you later if I need to." He never asked me about the runaway again. Incidentally, I did know the precise location that the boy had planned to go. He had never gotten there. He was found several days later and returned to Lyman.

At Lyman Hall, a boy was expected to adjust to the environment within the first month, and then be transferred to another cottage. If you were reasonably well-adjusted by the end of the first month, you earned 100 credits. A perfect score for subsequent months at other cottages earned one 125 credits per month. In this way, it would take me about six months to earn the 700 credits required for me to be released.

The daily schedule involved an unvarying routine that started with our being awakened at six in the morning. We would immediately make our beds in the large dormitory unless it was Wednesday. On Wednesday, we changed the bedding, so we queued up in line to receive the clean sheets. Bed-wetters (and there were quite a few) changed their sheets daily and washed their own sheets. They were required to use a rubber mattress cover. If you did not fess up to being a bed-wetter and stained the mattress, you were punished just as for any other lie. I started out using a rubber mattress cover since I had occasionally wet my bed in the past. I found that I had developed enough control, though, so I never needed it, and by the time I was transferred to Worcester Cottage, I did not request or need one.

An inspection of all the beds was performed by the Cottage Master to ascertain that the "hospital" corners were square and the blanket was at the proper tension. When all was well, we walked down the iron spiral staircase to the basement room where we removed our nightshirts and queued up in line for a shower. The shower was brief, but warm. We were required to brush our teeth and, for the fortunate few, to shave, using a community razor.

You were allowed a limit of five minutes to sit on the hopper. You were expected to adjust yourself to the schedule, so that each, in turn, could use the facilities at the appropriate time. There were eight hoppers lined up in a row. They did not have any seats, so you had to sit carefully to prevent an embarrassing accident. After that, you went to your locker and dressed. Shoes were expected to remain shined at all times. Any marks or smudges that had accumulated over the evening were carefully dressed out with a shoeshine brush and rag. Most idle time was to be spent shining your shoes.

At precisely eight in the morning, we lined up for the short walk to the cafeteria. My first stay at Lyman started in the early spring, so it was a cold brisk walk to the cafeteria. At the cafeteria, we usually had a choice of hot or cold cereal, powdered eggs, real milk, coffee or tea (diluted with a lot of milk), bacon or Spam, and toast. You could have all that you wanted, but could *never* fail to eat all that you had taken. The food at Lyman was excellent for an institution of its size. We were not allowed to talk in the cafeteria.

After eating, one of the boys was assigned the duty of collecting and counting all the flatware. Other boys were assigned cleanup duty so that when each group from each cottage left, the tables used were as spotless as when the group arrived. We left the cafeteria and marched back to Lyman Hall.

The cigarettes

Back at the cottage, we had one hour's free time before we were to report for school or work detail. During this time, boys who had their parents' permission were given a cigarette to smoke. The boys' parents supplied most of the cigarettes used. Some were supplied by the state. These were the Airline brand. Boys who had violated some rule but really did not quite deserve the dollar were denied their rationed cigarette. This, too, was part of the positive reinforcement training. I had never smoked before, but since there was a question about who would be required to give the permission (I had come from a foster home), I started the habit. The daily ration was three per day, so I do not think it affected anybody's health very much. Furthermore, I reasoned, it gave the Masters something to deny me if I messed up a little, rather than resorting to the dollar.

Work detail

While at Lyman Hall, one did not attend school. School was for those who had been transferred to the other cottages. At ten o'clock, we queued up for outside work detail. Mr. Humphrey usually supervised the work detail. It involved mowing lawns, garden work, and groundskeeping. It was hard, continuous work. The break came precisely at twelve noon when we returned to the cottage to get ready for lunch. After cleaning up and shining our shoes, we queued up in line and marched off to the cafeteria for lunch.

Lunch usually was quite good. There were salads, processed meats, and lots of milk and (weak) coffee. Many complained about the food at Lyman, but I found that it was very good. I started to gain weight and become very strong. When I first arrived at Lyman, I could barely push a lawnmower, having been sick at the YSB, as well as being very thin. Soon I was finishing my area quickly and then helping in the other areas where younger boys were having trouble. The Lyman School song contained, amongst other things, disparaging remarks about the food.

> They say up at Lyman,
> The coffee's mighty fine;
> It's used for cuts and bruises,
> They call it iodine.

I did not like the song. The food was great.

After lunch, we reported to the cottage and had another cigarette and an hour-long break. Then it was outside, back to work on the work detail. At dusk, or five o'clock, whichever came first, we returned to the cottage. After cleaning up and shining our shoes, we reported to the cafeteria again, precisely within our allocated time slot. The evening meal was the largest at Lyman except on Sunday. We usually had roast beef, baked ham, or some other meat with potatoes and vegetables. There was the usual milk and coffee or tea. Sometimes we had macaroni and cheese or baked beans, red kidney beans, or lima beans, but most often, we had good meat and potatoes.

> They say up at Lyman,
> The beans are mighty fine;
> But some jumped off the table,
> And shot a friend of mine.

After the evening meal, we marched back to the cottage and had our final cigarette for the day. After all our shoes were shined, and the basement was cleaned up, we were escorted upstairs to the dayroom on the second floor. This room had several tables, kept in immaculate condition by the houseboys, and a television set. I will tell more about the houseboys later.

We were allowed to play cards, write letters, read, and watch television. I did not watch very much television, since it made me think about the last TV show I viewed from an awkward position at the Youth Service Center. Instead, I read electronics books and magazines. I also drew schematics of various kinds of electronic equipment that I planned to build someday. Practically every scrap of paper that I could get my hands upon became another electronic adventure.

At nine o'clock, we returned to the basement to get ready for bed. Everybody wore a white nightshirt. They were all the same size, so on some they looked like a sack that hung to the floor. At precisely nine-thirty, we marched upstairs to the dormitory and went to bed. There's not much to say about the dormitory except that it was a very large room, contained fifty or more beds, was always cold in the winter, hot in the summer, and was attended by a guard who stayed in a little entryway office and either drank from a whiskey bottle, slept with his feet on the desk, or both. Incidentally, the guard was probably employed for Fire Code reasons; that is, some adult supervisor had to be on duty during the nighttime. I never saw a guard that was awake long enough to actually guard anything! Houseboys would sometimes sit outside on the fire escape in the heat of the summer and talk until well into the early morning hours. The guards would never even know it, busily snoring away. Generally, the houseboys watched over the cottages when the Cottage Masters were off duty. They did not touch any of the other inmates, only reporting any problems, which, to the best of my recollection, never occurred.

On Saturday, the routine was similar except that the afternoon work detail was replaced by movies. "Movies?" Yes, I said movies! We had a movie theater. Since I had seldom gone to the movies (almost never), this was a great experience for me! The movies were mostly "westerns" with an appropriate share of gunfire and violence. They were full-length, 35-millimeter films shown with a modern RCA carbon arc projector. The auditorium had a large pull-down screen covering the entire stage. Sometimes Mr. Kenney would address the boys in the auditorium after the movie. He would talk about things he was planning to do to make conditions better at the school. I thought conditions were already great.

On Sunday, instead of the morning work detail, we went to church. The auditorium was used for separate Catholic and Protestant services. We had an organ, hymnals, and a chaplain. Reverend Brown did not officiate at the early services that I remember. I met him during my later months at Lyman and really got to know him when I returned to Lyman the second time.

Visiting hours were from one until four o'clock in the afternoon on Sunday. Many boys never had any visitors at all. My parents came every Sunday. It was a lot easier for them to visit me at the Lyman School than at the YSB. My folks brought me candy bars and more reading material. I always wanted more paper, pens, and drafting equipment. They brought me what I wanted. They knew that I was getting along well at the school. My parents thought that I was a real pig since I usually ate one of the candy bars while they were present. I did not want them to know I was giving the stuff away. The fact is that those were the only candy bars that I ate. After they left, I would always divvy up my stuff among my friends who did not have any visitors. Most of my friends never had any visitors. I was their only link with the outside. I acquired these friends, not because I was altruistic and pure, but because I enjoyed being needed, appreciated, and loved. I needed those boys more than they needed me. Those candy bars were a cheap price to pay.

You have probably heard that everybody confined to a prison, reformatory, detention center, or training school claims that, of course, they are not guilty. Somehow they were framed, or, "The cops picked up the wrong person!" I do not know where this misinformation comes from because, after spending some considerable time in two of these institutions, I never heard anybody claim that they did not do whatever it was that they were supposed to have done. They may have made such complaints, but certainly not to other inmates. Instead, their complaints centered upon abuse—physical, emotional, and sometimes sexual. Most everybody thought that he had gotten a bad deal and, in fact, considering how the Massachusetts juvenile court system worked at the time, he probably had.

To give an example, when somebody is suddenly confined, it is possible for that person to encounter the same kinds of emotions that he might encounter after a death in his family. One of the first such emotions is denial. However, this is not the denial of the deed, but rather the denial that such a bad thing could be happening to him. This is a direct result of the confinement, and it goes away quickly as the prisoner begins to cope and adjust. Eventually the inmate begins to identify with his captors, perhaps as in the Stockholm syndrome. Anything that prevents the inmate from bonding with his captors may result in problems with adjustment. The persons who are controlling the security, that is, one's captors, such as the Masters or guards, must not be too abusive, or it will make their jobs very difficult as the inmates fail to adjust to their daily routines.

At the Lyman School, the Cottage Masters that I encountered were highly skilled and were able to accelerate adjustment by being just strict enough so the inmate was controlled, but also they could detect a likable person just below the surface. Personally, I never had any adjustment problems. I was well liked by both the Masters and the other inmates, and got along just fine. In fact, the Lyman School was so much better than the other places I had been, that once I got through the Lyman Hall indoctrination, I thoroughly enjoyed my stay!

Even though the accidental burning of a barn was not a crime and I should not have been charged with the crime of arson, I had been trained to accept responsibility for my actions. The Lyman School seemed to me to be the correct place for me to make recompense. If I could have gone there without first encountering the Youth Service Board Detention Center, I would not have encountered any emotional trauma at all. As it was, the YSB made my life quite a bit more difficult, but this is not a "woe is me" book. Instead, it is a book about what we had and, I truly believe, what we still need.

15

Worcester Cottage

After my first month, I transferred to Worcester Cottage. The Cottage Master and Matron were Mr. and Mrs. McCabe. I got along well there. I attended and did very well at the on-campus school. The classes were really at the sixth-grade level, but they were called the tenth grade. My after-school work first involved working with the janitor detail. We

Worcester Cottage

spent many hours cleaning and polishing the many floors of the school building, the cafeteria, and the recreation center. I attracted many friends. It seemed that just about everybody liked me. This was surprising to me because I had very few friends on the outside. I also liked just about everybody I met and worked with. During the work detail, you could talk with your friends as long as it did not interfere with your work. One of my friends became very close. I will talk about him a bit later.

I continued to become healthier because of the good food and the exercise, not only from work, but also from sports activity. I continued to grow and was no longer the proverbial 98-pound weakling.

Some of our free time was spent in sports. We had a basketball court and a softball diamond. I played both games and, even though on the outside I had never been allowed by my peers to play baseball, on the inside I excelled. I was not strong enough to hit a ball much out of the infield, but I learned that if I swung slowly and watched the incoming ball, I could always make contact and usually put the ball over the pitcher's head between first and second. This would get me on base. Since we competed between cottages, the Cottage Masters would always arrange the lineup for the most favorable advantage. I was usually put just before a power-hitter. Even if he made a crazy swing, I could usually be counted upon to steal second base. I could run like a rabbit. I was Worcester Cottage's not-so-secret weapon.

I had the same advantages in basketball. I could not hit the side of a wall with the ball, but I could run and dribble like crazy. I always played the entire game since I was so good at getting the ball to center. I learned quite a lot about teamwork at Lyman. I was living proof that if you gave a klutz the right job to do as part of a team, the team would win, not in spite of the klutz, but because of him!

Another rape

A man we called Button (behind his back), with reference to the size of his observed physical equipment, monitored the gym and swimming pool. I was told I shouldn't use his real name. He was a creep. When boys would swim at the pool, they were naked. Button would sit behind a small window in the wall and masturbate while watching the boys. Since I was on the janitor's crew, I knew quite well about this, because we had to clean the semen off the wall and floor.

My friend and I were working on janitor duty, and it was our task to sweep and mop the corridor between the auditorium and the gym. Boys who had proven themselves as capable and trustworthy workers usually needed no direct supervision. The corridor led to a long ramp with a roll-up door at its bottom. As long as the roll-up door was closed, this was just about the most private area in the whole school. My friend and I had often gone to this area to do some private things, which I will detail in a moment. This was after we had properly finished our job, and were not expected to report for another fifteen or twenty minutes.

Suddenly the roll-up door was ripped open and there stood Button—naked. "Aha," he said," I caught you two!" He grabbed my friend by the ears and forced his penis into my friend's mouth. I cried for him to stop. I knew that my friend had never done anything like that before. For me, it was different. I had survived this before. I grabbed Button's penis and put it in my mouth. I kept pumping as I heard my friend retch and gag. Finally, Button was finished as I gagged on the sour slime that lined my throat. Button said, "Nice boy…thank you very much." He rolled down the door and went away. I vomited. At least my ass was not in a sling like before.

The private things we had come to do were to write a letter to my friend's mother. He could not read or write. I often read his mother's letters to him at this place. He was my very first black friend.

The prizefight

Sometimes arguments would flare up between two boys. If the argument was not settled quickly, or if it looked as though fists were about to start flying, the argument would be settled upon the ancient field of battle. We all assembled in the basement locker room, where the contestants would put on fifteen-ounce boxing gloves. These were big and heavy. The rules were simple:

The fight would start with a bell and would end with a bell. There were no "rounds." Each would fight until the bell rang. The Cottage Master would ring the starting bell. Either contestant could ring the ending bell. Whoever rang the ending bell acknowledged that he had lost the fight. Either contestant could stop the fight by agreeing with the other to stop fighting, in which case it was a draw. If you hit the other contestant when he was down, you lost. You got ten dollars on the hand for bad sportsmanship.

My fight started when I called another boy a name. I did not really mean what I had said. It just came out wrong. The other boy, who was black, was furious and started swinging. I really should not have called him a pickaninny, but I did not know what it meant! I thought a pickaninny was a Negro boy with curly hair! I remembered that word from some piano sheet music I had played, *Stay in Your Own Back Yard.* It was in the piano bench when my father got the old piano from my great-grandmother. In the days before the Civil Rights movement, nobody used the word "black" to describe a person and "African American" was unheard of as well.

I had never used boxing gloves before. They were so heavy, I could hardly hold up my hands. The first time I was hit with one, I realized that it was also unlikely that I would get hurt; it was more like a pillow fight than a boxing match. Since I was well matched for size with my opponent, I figured it was unlikely that I would hurt him either. Here were these two boys with heavy pillows strapped to their hands, swinging wildly at each other, wearing each other out. I decided that I had two choices: either ask him for a draw, or just stand there covering up until he wore himself out. He refused the draw, so I just put both gloves to my cheeks and waited. After a fury of punches by my opponent that did absolutely nothing, even though they all connected with my unprotected torso, I dropped my gloves to my side, backed up, and let loose with one tremendous roundhouse right, as if I were pitching a baseball.

The swing only hit his arm, but the momentum of the heavy glove was enough to spin him rapidly around and land him on his butt. I stepped back as he slowly got to his feet. He turned, walked over to the Master's desk, and rang the bell. When we were having our gloves removed, I asked him why he gave up. "Hell," he said, "I don't want to know how it'd be if you ever *hit* me!" I liked him. We became good friends.

The batteries

One of my friends from Oak Cottage needed some batteries for his radio. I had met this person while sitting on the bench during one of our intercottage softball games. He had a radio that needed some batteries to make it work. His sister had visited him when he first came to Lyman and had brought him the radio. He used the radio until the batteries wore out but, since he no longer had any visitors, there was nobody on the "outs" that could bring him some batteries. I thought it a shame that he had a nice brand new transistor radio that he would carry everywhere with him (it was his only possession), but it would not work for lack of batteries.

There were some batteries at Worcester Cottage. They were used for Mr. McCabe's flashlight that he always kept handy in case the lights should go off. Many portable radios in those days required two kinds of batteries, an "A" battery, and a "B" battery. My friend's transistor radio was a new kind that only required flashlight batteries, but lots of them. It required eight! I stole a set of batteries and gave them to my friend.

When Mr. McCabe discovered that the batteries were missing, he gathered us together and said, "Somebody has stolen some batteries. You will all be punished until the thief admits what he has done." The punishment required that we all go upstairs and shine the floors. We each used a shine brush and, down on our hands and knees, we would shine the wooden floors until one could see his face in it. We would do this repeatedly. After working for about an hour, I admitted to Mr. McCabe that I had stolen the batteries.

"Where are the batteries?" asked the Cottage Master. "I gave them to a friend." I responded. "A friend? Now let me get this straight, you stole my batteries and gave them to a friend?" he bellowed. "Yes," I said, "he never gets any visitors, so he couldn't get any batteries. I just had to get some batteries for him. I'm sorry. I thought you had lots of batteries and wouldn't miss them much." Mr. McCabe had me sit up on my knees in the middle of the floor while he went and searched my locker.

Sitting up on one's knees was a standard punishment. Your knees would begin to hurt very soon. When he returned, Mr. McCabe let me get off my knees. Everybody was able to stop shining the floor and go back downstairs to the locker room. Mr. McCabe no doubt discovered that my locker contained no valuables, just some half-written letters that I had been helping some boys write to their parents. The alternate Cottage Master, Mr. De Martino, called me "Robin Hood" for a few weeks after the incident.

The poem

After my brush with Lyman School's law, I did a lot of thinking about the incident and what, if anything, it meant. I realized that I had developed a very strange code of honor. I would do anything for a friend, even steal, or prostitute myself, but I could never even think of doing anything like that for myself! One day in the TV room upstairs, I put aside my notebook of electronic schematics and wrote a poem.

The Robin

I was wandering down this lonely road,
And I saw a robin fly;
I'd often seen this same old bird,
So high up in the sky;

I asked him how come his feathers,
Shed so easily all the rain;
And why he sang so beautifully,
In the morning up the lane;

I asked him if he ever got angry,
As he saw the morning sun;
Of if he ever just loafed around,
Until the day was done;

Then finally I asked him,
If he ever told a lie;
I listened to his answers,
And they almost made me cry;

"You see, boy," said the robin,
"I don't really like to sing;
But God said I'd have to do it,
So the people'd know it's spring;

"And the feathers on my back,
As you can surely see;
You have a finer coat,
Than God ever gave to me;

"If I ever got angry,
Well, I surely do;
But I vowed when I was created,
To never be blue;

"If I ever loafed around,
Until the day was done;
I've done that lots of times,
And had a lot of fun;

"But if I ever told a lie,
I don't think I ever could;
'Cause cross my heart and hope to die,
God made me to be good."

We can look at this and muse, a very amateur poem. Nevertheless, in fact, it represents some very deep thinking on the part of a fourteen-year-old boy. I found at Lyman that most of the boys thought much more of others than they did of themselves. Many had gotten into trouble with the law because they started working against a system that was all wrong and was hurting their friends. I never heard anybody bragging about his or her crimes. I only heard remorse, not necessarily for doing some bad thing, but for being caught. Most were caught because they were very moral persons who refused to lie or compromise their principles. A very wise Lyman School boy once told me that you never have to remember what you told somebody if you always told the truth.

Later on, I recited this poem to an English teacher at Westborough High School. She said it was, in fact, a sonnet with a few lines more than the requisite 14 of iambic pentameter. I knew nothing about poetry when I wrote this. It just seemed to sound okay.

16

The Summer Trades

School was out for the summer, just like on the outs. We did not spend our time sleeping in the shade. All the boys were to learn a trade in the various trade shops at the facility. Those who were too dense to learn a trade ended up working as groundskeepers. My first trade assignment was in the carpentry shop. The school was a complete city within  itself. All building maintenance and repair was done by the carpentry shop. The cafeteria, of course, handled the feeding of five hundred or more residents. The laundry did its job and then, of course, there was the farm.

The best of all trades was carried on in the print shop. In that shop, nearly all of the official documents and stationery for the state of Massachusetts was typeset and printed. I wanted to work in the print shop, but there was a long waiting list of boys who had excelled in other trades and were waiting for an opening to occur. Instead, I went to work in the carpentry shop. The Master of the carpentry shop was Mr. McPherson. He was a very temperamental man. The boys called him "Turkey" behind his back.

> They say up at Lyman,
> The work is mighty fine;
> It's used for keeping busy,
> You do it all the time.

I did very well at the carpentry shop. I had always been very capable when using hand tools. I also took great pride and care with my work. One of my first jobs was to help repair an ancient wooden window that had been broken. The frame itself had been broken in several places where the wood had rotted out. Mr. McPherson was a very capable carpenter. He usually used the boys under his charge for the grunt work, while he carefully restored intricate bric-a-brac himself. He had carefully cut out the rotted pieces from the frame and fashioned new pieces from his memory of what they should look like.

My task was to remove all the old paint from the frame so it could be reglazed and repainted like new. He told me how to remove the paint, gave me a few crude hand tools, and some sandpaper, and went on to other tasks. I labored for several hours, removing all the paint. I sanded and smoothed the surface until there were no green stains from the fifty-year-old paint that had covered the sash for as many winters. When he returned Mr. McPherson said, "Haven't you finished that goddamn window yet?" I told him I was almost done.

He walked over, took a quick look at my work, hesitated with his mouth open like he was just about to yell at me again, and then said, "My God! We've finally found a goddamn carpenter!" This was my first and last compliment from Mr. McPherson. I knew he liked my work because I usually got the jobs that required skill rather than brawn. It just was not in Mr. McPherson's nature to offer any compliments. However, he was an extremely skillful carpenter. I was amazed at the work that he did. He could have taught me a lot. He was also a very demanding man. I liked the work, though. I would have stayed in the carpentry shop if it were not for Mr. McPherson's temper.

The beating

Mr. McPherson was a man of very small stature. He always had at least one inmate working for him who was as large and brutal as they come. The inmate was somewhat of a line boss, the man second in charge. The bouncer at the time I worked in the shop was a 200-pound brute with a Polish name who barely spoke or understood English.

I had just returned from the infirmary building after painting some wood trim when Mr. McPherson demanded to know why it had taken so long. I told him that I was trying to do the job properly, so it took a little longer. He said, "You think you can come and go around here as you damn well please. You figure you've got it made around here 'cause I put a goddamn paintbrush in your hand 'stead of a goddamn spade."

Pointing to me, Mr. McPherson told his bouncer, "Go get that sonabitch!" The Neanderthal responded with a lunge that sent me sprawling on the floor. Then he sat on my chest and beat me on the face until I had blood running from every orifice. "Turkey" just walked away as I was continually pummeled. Using my small frame to a slight advantage, I wiggled free, ran outside, and continued down to the administration building.

> They say up at Lyman,
> The Masters mighty fine;
> One flew off the handle,
> And beat a friend of mine.

The man in charge

This was the first time I had ever been to the AB. I saw a secretary near the front door and I told her that I must see Mr. Kenney. Mr. Kenney was the assistant superintendent. I sat in a wicker chair and wiped the blood from my face with my shirt. Soon Mr. Kenney appeared. He asked me to come into his office, closed the door behind me, then asked, "And what may I do for you?"

I told him what had happened and he asked, "What do you think? I have got over five hundred boys here. Do you think that all I've got to do is to play nursemaid to every kid who comes barging in here just because he's got a little problem?" "No," I said, "I just don't want to get beaten up anymore. I know you care about what goes on, so I figured you should know since Mr. McPherson's probably reported me as a runaway by now." Mr. Kenney picked up the phone and asked me to step outside his office. In a few minutes, he opened his office door and asked what my name was. I told him and he returned to his office and closed the door behind him again.

In a few more minutes, Mr. Kenney returned from his office and said, "Go over to the infirmary and get fixed up, and tomorrow report to the print shop." I was elated. I said, "Oh thank you so very, very, much." He interrupted, "Go on now…get out of here."

I was pretty banged up and I had several broken teeth. The nurse at the infirmary, Mrs. Tremblay, was familiar with my work since I had been there painting less than an hour before. She inquired, "Is this what Turkey did to you for your super carpentry work?" I nodded. She already knew.

The print shop

Mr. Burden was the print shop Master. He was a very reserved, quiet, and kindly man. A very patient teacher, he took great pride in the work of his boys. He always made them feel as though they were very important. He wanted them all to become great printers. Printing was a very noble trade. "Benjamin Franklin was a printer," he kept reminding us.

The type was set by hand. We learned kerning and blocking, started to think about sizes in picas, and ran the presses. Mr. Burden had shaking palsy. His hands were in constant motion. However, when he would hold a chassis and start setting type, the shaking stopped and was replaced by exquisite precision, as he would lay type as fast as I could read the copy. As I watched him one day he joked, "You could do this too, but your hands shake too much!" Because I was a good reader, Mr. Burden would usually ask me to read the copy after he had first reviewed it.

He could set type at about ten to twelve words per minute when somebody was reading. At that rate, his fingers were flying, almost like playing the piano. After the initial setting of type, Mr. Burden would take a lot of time kerning the type and adjusting everything so it looked perfect. He would ink a squeegee and make a single imprint on a sheet of paper. He would first read the copy, and then he would pass it around, so that every pair of eyes in the print shop could look for errors. It was only after the first chassis was free of errors that he would set type for any subsequent page. This is how he taught the boys a work ethic that would serve them for a lifetime, even if they did not all become printers as he wished.

Running the presses was quite boring. You would stand for hours swapping sheets of paper in precise synchronism with the machine. Should you get careless, or get out of step, you could lose your hand. I never saw any accidents at the print shop because everyone in my group had been properly taught to respect the machine. At the end of a run, we would disassemble and clean the presses, then carefully reassemble and oil them. Most of the machines were truly ancient, but all appeared as new and sparkling as on the day they were installed fifty or more years before.

One of the advantages of working at the print shop was that the work came in bunches. We would have to work very rapidly with much concentration for several days, and then we would have a few days just to hang around. I used the slack time to learn how to unlock locks without keys. We did not break into anything; we just tried to open locks for sport! The unofficial name of the print shop became the "Locksmith." When a Cottage Master had forgotten the combination of a padlock for his kid's bicycle, or wanted to get a lock on a doorknob from his home fixed, he would bring it over and let us work on it. Locksmithing had nothing to do with printing, but at Lyman, it came with the territory.

The chaplain

I used some of my slack time to do some exploring. Officially, we were not allowed away from the print shop during working hours, but all you had to do was let Mr. Burden know where you were going, and he would cover for you.

I used my knowledge of locksmithing to gain access to the auditorium. This was where the movies were shown on weekends and where Sunday services were held. The auditorium contained a Hammond organ. I just had to play it. I had learned to play the piano as a youngster, but I had given it up about a year or two before my troubles at home had started. I taught myself to play that organ. Organs were not like pianos. It was not very easy.

One morning I was aggressively playing a hymn from the church hymnal. There was no other written music around, so I would play all the hymns that we would sing on Sunday morning. I would also throw in a few variations now and then, playing odd chord sequences, and then trying to work myself out of the musical mess into which I had gotten myself.

After a particularly difficult passage, in which I changed keys several times, but was able to get back to the original without any discords, I looked up and Reverend Brown, the Protestant chaplain, was sitting in the front row of the otherwise empty auditorium. I had just been caught playing the organ without permission. Reverend Brown did not seem to care! He stood up and applauded. He introduced himself and asked that I stop by his office sometime.

Bob Brown's office became a regular hangout for me and a few other boys. He never threw religion at us. We would talk about anything and everything. It was just great to go there and shoot the bull. This person was great. Everybody wanted to be like Reverend Brown. He liked to do neat stuff for no good reason at all, just like the kids. Even though he seemed to think the way we did, he was always correct and proper. He was never crude or coarse. Later he would arrange for his groupies to take trips off campus. Since I had not yet earned all 700 credits that I needed, I was not quite privileged enough to hang around as a groupie all the time. That would come later. For now, I just played his organ and dropped by to chat. Eventually the boy who played the organ during church services would finish his sentence and go home. I would become the next church organist.

The houseboys

By the middle of summer, I had finally earned my 700 credits. I should have been able to go home, but it was not quite that simple! Earning 700 credits, it seemed, only made me eligible for parole. I was not going to go home until quite some time later. Boys who had done their time were sometimes promoted to the rank of houseboy. The word houseboy has recently become perverted. Do not think for a moment that Lyman School houseboys were anything like those described on the Internet! Houseboys had many privileges. They also, as the name implied, worked around the house. I was one of the lucky ones promoted to houseboy.

Typically, the houseboys would work upstairs with the Matron cleaning the rooms, shining the tables, and generally doing housework. We were also the messengers to deliver and receive the mail. Although there was a massive laundry for cleaning the boys' clothing and bedding, houseboys washed the stockings every day. We also cleaned the showers and toilets. This might not sound like too much of a promotion, but in return for our work, we received respect and extra cigarettes. We were trusted to go anywhere on campus without supervision. We were also allowed to do other things that might earn us some money or cigarettes.

I repaired car radios for Cottage Masters and their friends. I also washed and waxed automobiles, as did other houseboys. Once, Reverend Brown arranged for a Westborough Police car to come to Lyman so I could attempt to fix a police radio that had been giving the police radio repair depot a lot of trouble. I traced the problem to a broken shield from the antenna's coaxial cable. I remember pointing out the problem to Reverend Brown after I found it: "See, it takes two wires to conduct electricity!" was my explanation when I discovered that the coaxial cable shield was not bonded to the car's body.

In time, word got out, and I was even recruited to look at some State Police radios that were providing poor performance. In every case the coaxial cable leading to the antenna had an open shield and was not bonded to the car body at the feed-through to the antenna itself.

Learning that I was able to fix electronic equipment, Mr. Kenney asked me to look at his television. This was not the big color TV in his living room. Instead, it was a small black-and-white TV in his bedroom. I discovered that it needed a pair of selenium rectifiers. I asked Mr. Kenney to stop by the TV repair shop in town and get a pair of silicon rectifiers to replace the obsolete and worn out selenium units. I asked Mr. Sandini for his soldering equipment. The following day, I returned to Mr. Kenney's house and completed the repair. The television "worked better than when brand-new," Mr. Kenney said. Later on, I would get to fix his color TV.

> They say up at Lyman,
> The houseboys' mighty fine;
> Used to making trouble,
> And loafing all the time.

Mr. Sandini, the Master at Westview Cottage, started an amateur radio club. Many houseboys attended, but I was the only one who already had a ham license. I taught Morse code. I also spent a lot of time talking on the six-meter ham station that Mr. Sandini had donated.

Since I was being considered a candidate for parole, I was required to report once a week to Miss Pazian, the school psychologist. The school also had another psychologist who took several houseboys off campus to watch drive-in movies at times. Miss Pazian did her duty and asked me all the questions necessary to fill in the boxes in her forms. One question I remember seemed a bit too personal for a woman to ask. I asked her if it was all right if I kept one or two secrets to myself.

She said, "I don't ever want you to tell me anything that you think could hurt you. Some things that might hurt you now may, in the future, not cause you any harm so you might want to tell somebody then, but as far as I know it's good to have a few secrets."

It sure made me feel good that I did not have to tell her everything. She never knew about the rocket or any of my personal experiences in the past. She knew that I had many secrets, but she also did not let that stand in the way of my parole. I respected her for that.

The school had a weekend program where those who were going to be sent home on parole were allowed to visit their families over the weekend several times. This was supposed to help the boys adjust from the intensely regimented atmosphere at Lyman to the new home environment. I visited my new home in New Braintree and was very excited about going home. My father seemed to share the excitement, but my mother was very reserved. My two sisters spent many hours asking me questions about the Lyman School and what it was like.

When the time was approaching that I should leave Lyman School for the promised new life in New Braintree, I would lie awake at night in the dormitory watching the rats scurry across the intricate bridgework that supported the roof. The lights were always illuminated in the dormitory and reflected off the open-truss ceiling. I would watch the furry little grey creatures as they darted about, doing whatever rats do. Somebody would stir, and a rat would halt in a heartbeat, maintaining its invisible position until it was assured that the movement below had ceased.

I wondered how many generations of rats had lived in Worcester Cottage. I wondered if they would survive if they were suddenly transported to a new environment like New Braintree. Probably not, I thought. Nevertheless, certainly the rats had been able to adjust from the conditions that existed when meals were served in the cottages, to the present when meals were served at the cafeteria. Where did they get their food now? Did they make little nighttime trips to the cafeteria and bring back some bounty for their families?

The rats obtained their livelihood not only by becoming invisible to all but those who had discovered their nighttime habitat, but also by being flexible.

While survival on the outs didn't involve becoming invisible, I needed to become flexible, just like the rats.

REFLECTIONS

The Lyman School Tower

Oh sturdy steel who stands so tall,
To guard the hill night and day;

Like a mother hen she guards her flock,
From trouble along the way;

This tower seen for miles around,
Spread out beneath her skirt;

These boys who came from far away,
Where they had felt the hurt;

No harm will come to her children,
While she is standing tall;

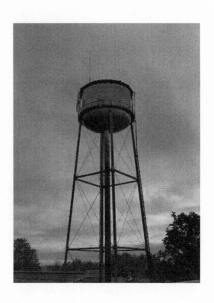

She watches and she listens,
To the boys at Lyman Hall;

In early morn I see her weep,
She's burdened so with care;

She knows that many of her boys,
Will again some trouble bear.

As the morning sun dries her tears,
She smiles and looks at me;

For I shall be her happy child,
As soon I will be free.

17

Going Home

The Lyman School tower did cry as the early morning mist condensed against her cold steel. In the hot days of August when the lawns were turning brown, I remember it well—she cast a green shadow from her morning tears.

Mr. Borys himself told me I was going home. He said that I had been one his best students and that he was proud of me. He warned me about the trials I would encounter in the future and wished me the best.

When I went to the clothes storage room to get my civilian clothes, I discovered that I had grown much too big for them. Mr. Ferguson, the man in charge, said, "Not to worry." He presented me with the best of the

New Braintree

newest clothes that he could find from the Lyman School supplies. I looked and felt sharp. I joined my parents at the AB and my father drove me to my new home.

> Gee ma, I wanta go,
> Back where the flowers grow;
> Gee ma, I wanta go home.

Home was now New Braintree, a small town about fifteen miles from North Brookfield. My parents had rented a small farmhouse after they had lost the farm in North Brookfield. My mother was furious that I had started smoking cigarettes and she was deathly afraid that I might attack my two sisters. To her, I was the black sheep of the family. I was evil through-and-through. She told me so. I did not have any money to purchase cigarettes anymore, even at 25 cents per pack, so I had to give up smoking.

My new home in New Braintree seemed worse than the work farm in Barre. I attended school in Gilbertville, which required a long school bus ride. I bought a used bicycle and rode it about two miles to and from the school bus stop each morning and evening. It was an old-style bicycle with balloon tires. I was able to buy it for five dollars from a classmate who had just gotten a ten-speed.

Most students in New Braintree attended the new regional high school in North Brookfield as my sisters did. I was not allowed to attend that school because Mr. Leach, the superintendent, refused my admission, claiming that I was a known juvenile delinquent. It did not make any difference whether or not this discrimination was legal. Even nondelinquent juveniles did not have any rights in Massachusetts at the time.

Before school, I chopped wood for the stove. After school, I worked in the barn. My father had begun studying for the ministry, so he arranged for me to wind the church clock every weekend. This was not easy. It took about two hours of my time and thoroughly prevented the possibility of any social life on weekends. My father seemed quite proud of my strength and ability. He even loaned me to a local farmer to help harvest hay. I never got any pay for the subsequent sixteen-hour weekends.

The teachers at Gilbertville High had been told that I was a genius and had all the makings of a great scientist. In an attempt to help me become a future scientist, the physics department enrolled me in a college-level physics correspondence course. The work was very hard, but I did well. However, I failed most of my regular high school courses. The teachers had assumed that, since I was very smart, I wanted to become another Einstein. They never asked me what I wanted to be. In fact, I wanted to be an ordinary kid who played baseball after school.

I was isolated from my classmates and friends again. This was a very lonely time for me. I longed to talk to my friends who remained at Lyman. I tried to telephone a friend from Bridgewater who had been paroled about a month before me. My mother caught me using the telephone, and I was never allowed to use my parents' telephone again. Instead, I broke into the municipal garage and called my friend from the telephone inside. As I talked to my friend, I discovered that he, too, had the same problems as me. We were both isolated from our friends and were very confused and lonely. Being on the outside was no longer where we wanted to be.

It's interesting that, although Lyman School was the first, and perhaps the only, home that many boys had, and the friends that the boys made at Lyman were often the only friends that they ever had, they were not allowed to communicate, or associate, with these friends after they had completed their Lyman School stay. I was told that this was the law. However, as was with most such laws having to do with juvenile delinquents in the fifties and sixties, I was never able to find any such written codification. Probation and parole officers, police, and judges just made up laws as they went along. I suppose that if two brothers were paroled from the Lyman School they would not be able to talk to each other for the rest of their lives!

There are some strange laws the state of Massachusetts still has on its books. For example, "Chapter 272: Crimes against chastity, morality, decency, and good order." Think about that for a moment! Being unchaste is a crime in the state of Massachusetts, as is being out of order. Although such laws are not usually enforced, they can be. They remain on the books apparently so there is always something that the police can use to harass and intimidate. I learned about the being out of order law later, when I wanted to stay inside the Boston Public Library to read a book the librarian would not let me take home. Nevertheless, in spite of all the strange laws on the books, there is nothing about parolees associating with other parolees. In fact, such laws would be unworkable. There could not be any halfway houses if parolees could not associate with each other, so it seems as though the phony law was falsely promulgated just to keep parolees from having any friends.

One weekend I rode my bicycle to Barre to try to find Wendell and Billy. Wendell was home, but he no longer considered me a friend. He would talk only for a few minutes, and then he left me alone in his yard. I guess that once one graduated from reform school you were marked as garbage forever. The rumors about my sudden departure from Barre High School had been that I torched the entire institution, leaving all the boys out in the cold, as some kind of revenge. I discovered that the physics teacher who had helped me build my rocket promulgated this rumor. Apparently, he was covering his butt at my expense. Billy was no longer at Stetson. Nobody knew where he had gone. I sat down by the side of the road and cried. I wanted to hold Billy in my arms just one more time. Why did he go away? Why was he taken away from me? He could have been the little brother I never had. I would have been his big brother who would protect him forever. If I could only find him, nobody could ever hurt us again. It was my fifteenth birthday.

I still had one friend on the outs though. He lived in North Brookfield and he was an amateur radio operator as well. Even though I had a radio license, I had never been able to get on the air. I just could not find the right radio parts in trashcans to get my transmitter working. My friend's name was Skip Anderson. Just about every time I was able to sneak away from home, I would ride my bicycle the fifteen miles to North Brookfield to visit him. He was interested in lasers. They represented the latest state of the art of technical achievement. He was going to make one for the science fair. His major problem was getting a ruby crystal. He was very smart and had made a xenon flash-tube exciter. He would have made the whole laser had it not been for the considerable problem of finding a cheap ruby.

I told him that I knew how to make a laser gyroscope, and that maybe I would make one some day for my science fair project. When I was sent back to Lyman, I gave him all my electronic treasures I had saved from TV repair shop trashcans.

One day after the summer harvest, while I was supposed to be attending school in Gilbertville, I walked all the way to Ware, Massachusetts. When I got into town, I saw a radio and television repair shop, the Ware Radio Service. I walked in and asked for a job. Mr. Belcher, the owner of the store, asked me a couple of questions about superheterodyne techniques used in radios and television sets. I promptly responded with the correct answers and got a job working on the bench on Saturdays. My mother was furious with me, but my father did not think it was such a bad thing for me to do. My father took me to work in Ware on Saturdays and Mr. Belcher brought me back home after work. Although I did not make much money at the shop, my work was good enough so Mr. Belcher did not mind driving me the ten miles back home every weekend.

18

Returning to Lyman School

My parole officer came every month. He knew I was not doing very well. My grades in school were very poor and my mother kept insisting that I was a menace to her home. She even invented stories about me stealing gallons of ice cream from her freezer. Although the parole officer knew I had done nothing wrong, he also knew that

things just were not working out. One day he came and told me he would have to take me back to Lyman. I told him I would be glad to go back, but I did not want to have to go to Oak Cottage which was the place that all the returnees go. "Couldn't you just bring me back to Worcester Cottage?" I asked. He said that he could not guarantee where I would go, but he felt sure that I would not be punished because he was bringing me back for replacement, not for violation of parole.

When I returned to Lyman School, I went directly to Oak Cottage just like any other returnee. Oak Cottage was where boys with disciplinary problems stayed. Many returnees had run away, or had been in various scraps at the institution. I was no different from other returnees, I was told by the Cottage Master. At Oak Cottage, the emphasis was on work. There was very little free time. We worked at menial physical tasks from early in the morning to late in the evening. The Lyman School farm had closed down, so we would go to the barnyard and dig holes as deep as one's height and as wide as one's outstretched arms. We would then fill them back in. I guess the idea was to keep everyone so busy that they did not have any time to get into trouble. It was actually relatively easy work once you found out where previous holes existed!

> They say up at Lyman,
> Oak Cottage is mighty fine;
> When they are not beating you,
> You're working all the time.

During my second week at Oak, Mr. Kenney, the assistant superintendent, called the Cottage Master at Oak, Mr. Jackman, and asked him to send me down to his house to repair his television. Mr. Jackman was quite surprised that Mr. Kenney called for me. He asked me how it was that I knew Mr. Kenney personally. I told him that we were friends from my previous stay and that he knew I was a good kid and had not done anything wrong.

I went to Mr. Kenney's house and checked out his television. It needed to have the tuner cleaned and a new tube installed. I gave him a list of parts that I needed, so he could get them the following day. While I was at his house, Mr. Kenney asked about how I had come to return to the Lyman School. His wife gave me a piece of cake with ice cream and a cup of coffee. Mr. Kenney said, "Don't worry too much. We'll get you out of Oak Cottage as soon as possible. You're there just because that's how the whole institution is set up. We don't have facilities to readmit kids directly into the other cottages."

I walked back to Oak Cottage feeling very much better. Lyman School had started to become a good place for me again. Two days later, I returned to Mr. Kenney's house to repair his television. It worked great. Mr. Kenney said, "We're trying to get you into Elms Cottage. How'd you like to go to Elms?" I told him that it was okay with me, but, "Not to worry, they're starting to treat me real good at Oak." In about a week, I transferred to Elms Cottage. The Cottage Master's name was Mr. Sherwood.

At Elms Cottage, there was a long list of boys waiting to be houseboys, so it was unlikely that I would be able to be one there. Mr. Sherwood said, "If you think you're going to be a privileged character here, you've got another thing coming. You're no different than all the others here, even though you think you've got the inside track with Mr. Kenney."

I found that most of the Masters would talk tough, but eventually they would show that they were nice people. Mr. Sherwood was no exception. He just wanted to show me that he was boss, after which he let me do just about anything I wanted. He learned that there was a houseboy opening at the administration building and he recommended me for the job.

Being a houseboy at the AB was like being the most trusted person in the whole school. No direct supervision existed for any of the tasks that had to be performed. There were only three of us, and our duties involved keeping the place immaculately clean and being available as a messenger. The outside work was completed by the grounds crews from Oak and Lyman Hall, so I did not have to do much hard work at all, except in the wintertime when we had to shovel snow. It was mandatory that the walks to the AB be cleaned before any of the AB staff arrived, so we needed to shovel before breakfast. Sometimes when I had little to do, I would stop by Miss Pazian's office and talk. Sometimes I would visit Mr. Borys or Mr. Kenney.

Most of my spare time was spent hanging around Reverend Brown's office. I played the organ for the Sunday services and even started to play another instrument.

The trombone

While exploring the old school building, I discovered a corner in the loft that contained many old band instruments. Most were destroyed beyond repair. I found a trombone that needed only a mouthpiece. It was greatly corroded, and would benefit from a good cleaning and shining, but otherwise it was in very good shape. I asked Reverend Brown if I could have it. He told me that he would check to see if I could. He thought that certainly it would be okay to use it, so I spent several days cleaning and polishing it. Reverend Brown brought me even better news. He said that not only could I use it, but also the school was going to hire a music teacher to teach me how to play it. Reverend Brown bought me a brand-new mouthpiece.

When the music teacher arrived, he started to show me how to play the scales. I produced a piece of sheet music and said, "To heck with the scales. Just help me mark the slide positions on this sheet, so I can play a real song." The music was *Red Sails in the Sunset*. The music teacher thought he would teach me that it was not going to be that easy, so he just marked up the first few bars. I started to play. The music teacher was very surprised that I was able to play the song. When I ran out of marked bars, he continued to tell me where the slide should be for the rest of the piece. Of course, by the time I got to the end, my unpracticed lip had given up, but the music teacher knew right away that I would be a very good student.

During the next few months, I learned to play many songs on that instrument. During one assembly, I played *The Star Spangled Banner* before the entire school. My ability to learn to play that instrument was the catalyst that allowed several other talented boys to be taught to play instruments by the new music teacher. I never had to practice scales.

19

Freedom on the Outside

Weekends away from Lyman School

Reverend Brown and his church in Westborough started a program where selected boys would be able to leave the Lyman School on Sundays and visit church members at their homes. The boys selected were those who had already done their time, but for reasons beyond their control, were unable to be paroled from the institution. The most common rea-

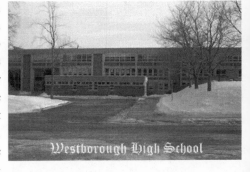

Westborough High School

son was that there just was not anywhere for them to go. Those who had come from poor home situations would need to go to foster homes. Most institution-type foster homes were already full and private homes were usually out of the question. The most common scenario was for these boys to stay at the institution until they were old enough to join the army or navy. Reverend Brown wanted to help change all that. As far as he was concerned, his boys from the school were good people who, by the accident of birth, arrived at the wrong place at the wrong time. He obtained permission for me to join the Alden family for Sunday dinner.

The Alden family lived in a nice house on a hill overlooking Westborough. At that time the hill, Fay Mountain, was called "Radar Mountain." A coastal defense surveillance radar installation overlooked their home. My first weekend away from the school was great. Mr. Alden was a consulting engineer working on a project to automate the U.S. Postal System. One of his projects involved counting the number of pieces of mail that passed a certain point in the system. He had designed a prototype that simulated the problem. He showed me a technical problem with the method of counting mail. The problem was that the mail would arrive at random times. This meant that, even if the average rate at which the mail arrived were constant, the counter-indicator would show a crooked line on the chart. He asked me what I thought about the problem. I matter-of-factly advised that he would have to integrate the data and promptly devised an electronic circuit to do it! I was only fifteen years of age at that time, so he was very impressed.

The Alden family liked me and I liked them. After several trial Sundays, I was allowed to stay the entire weekend with them. I spent almost every weekend at their home until I left the Lyman School.

Attending Westborough High School

The success of Reverend Brown's program led to new programs. Mr. Borys reasoned that if kids were well behaved enough to be allowed to visit families away from the Lyman School, then they were certainly capable of attending the learning institutions in town. The Lyman School had classes that went only to the ninth grade. If I was attending school, I should have been in the tenth grade. Mr. Borys made it happen. I do not know what strings he pulled, but soon I found myself a student in the tenth grade at Westborough High.

This was a brand-new regional high school and I liked it very much. The school bus would stop at the front entrance of Lyman School and bring me to the high school. Unless it was a very cold morning, I did not take the bus, preferring to walk the mile or so to school, so I could enjoy my newfound freedom. I was not a very good student—my grades were such that I just barely passed—but I was no problem for anybody at the school and I was liked by both the teachers and students.

After school, I would often walk through the town center on my way back to Lyman. I noticed that the TV repair company that had a contract at Lyman to maintain the television sets had a store downtown. The company's name was JJ TV and Appliances. One day I stopped by the store and talked to the owner. I told him that I was well qualified to repair not only televisions and radios, but also the kinds of two-way radios used in police and fire vehicles. I wanted him to give me a job on the weekends, so I would not have to spend too much of my time at Lyman.

He told me he would check it out to see if it was okay.

When I returned to Lyman, I went directly to the AB to talk to Mr. Kenney, so I could convince him to okay the after-school job. Neither he nor Mr. Borys were there at the time, so I walked up to Reverend Brown's office. He was not in either. I arrived late at the cafeteria and almost went without supper. When I returned to the cottage, the Master told me that it had been tentatively approved. I was elated! Everyone at Lyman School was pulling for me. I never had to wait for a decision to be made. Mr. Kenney and Mr. Borys just improvised. We were all in uncharted territory. I got whatever I wanted, and I never let them down.

20

Freedom on the Inside

Back to Lyman Hall and the Rubber Ducky antenna

I became the first (and last) boy ever to be transferred back to Lyman Hall. This was so I could come and go as my school and job required without affecting the schedules in other cottages. I was given use of a front office at Lyman Hall where I was supposed to do my homework. I spent most of my time there talking on my amateur radio set that I had built with parts donated by Mr. Sandini and the owner of the TV shop. My call was "K1KLR fixed-portable-one Lyman School." I operated on the six-meter phone band. My antenna was first a metal screen on a screen-door. Then I invented what eventually became known as the "Rubber Ducky" antenna.

After returning from outside school each afternoon, I was supposed to use a small room at the front of Lyman Hall for my homework studies. After barely completing my homework, I would set up my amateur radio station and attempt to communicate with others in the Westborough area. I didn't have a place to install an antenna, so I would connect the shield of a coaxial cable to the screen of a screen-door, poke the center conductor through a hole in the screen, then attach a 1/4 wavelength wire to that. This would dangle outside and sometimes work as an antenna.

Some amateurs would refer to this makeshift antenna as "loading up a screen-door." At one time, I thought I heard the words screen-door spring. This made me think. The problems with the wire dangling through the screen were that it was too long and it was not properly oriented for a good antenna.

My first attempt at a Rubber Ducky antenna was what I called the "Cantenna." The name was much later used by Heathkit to describe a dummy load. This consisted of a paint can filled with rocks for support. To the top of the can, I soldered four radials of brazing rod. Their length was determined by the size of the floor of the closet where I would store this contraption. In the center of the can's lid, I installed a coaxial connector so that the solder connection was oriented upward from the top of the can and outside the can. I punched a hole in the side of the can, so that I could insert the coaxial cable from the transmitter and receiver T/R relay. I soldered a section of a screen door spring to the center conductor of the coaxial connector.

I found that the spring needed to be only about ten inches high after I had stretched it so that none of the turns touched each other. This was tuned, with the transmitter at low power, by adjusting the length, so that a neon bulb would illuminate when brought near the top of the spring, and an inductive loop coupled to a light bulb would light the bulb when brought near the base of the spring. One strange anomaly was that the current flowing in the direction from the input connector towards the end far exceeded the current in the individual turns of the spring! This meant that the assembly seemed to fail to follow Ohm's law, where all currents in series must be the same.

After I scratched my eye while taking my portable antenna down, Mr. Sandini suggested that I put the spring inside a piece of windshield wiper hose. Since we didn't have shrink-tubing in those days, this was difficult to do. I tried threading a wire through the spring to pull the spring through the tubing from the bottom of the spring so it wouldn't distort and stretch out the antenna, and I finally succeeded.

Mr. Sandini carried out some further experiments with my antenna, such as making one that required no ground radials at all. It was just a spring in a rubber hose with a banana plug on one end. This would plug into the top antenna connector on the portable transceivers used by the Civil Defense, the Gonset Communicator III. He made several for both the six- and two-meter amateur radio bands. After using this antenna successfully at a Ham Fest in Swamscot, Massachusetts, Mr. Sandini published an article about it in the *QST* magazine, an amateur radio periodical. Mr. Sandini did give me some credit for the antenna, but he said that he was not allowed to use my name because I was a juvenile in a reform school. He had written, "A student from my code class at the training school designed the original antenna." The fact is that I was hardly a student in his code class. I was the instructor in his code class! I already knew Morse code. I was teaching code when Mr. Sandini was occupied with his amateur radio station.

This episode began a whole lifetime of events where I would do something useful and somebody else would claim credit for it or, as in this example, wouldn't use my name when describing the invention! Prior to my making that antenna, few seemed concerned in any way about the things I created, or the successes I had. They were fixated only upon my failures, perceived or actual. I show a modern version of my Rubber Ducky antenna attached to the handheld transceiver in the picture at the beginning of this chapter. Eventually I would invent even more complex and incredible things, usually because I was too uneducated to know that they could not work!

Now, neither Mr. Sandini nor I knew why the spring worked so well as an antenna. My first thought for the design was that I needed a spring that, when stretched out, would be 1/4 wavelength long to emulate a 1/4 wavelength whip. I carefully calculated the stretched-out length of a spring from its circumference and wire diameter. Imagine my surprise when I found out that the thing would resonate, produce an excellent match, and actually function as an antenna, at about 1/6 the calculated length! At the time it was thought that it was the resonance alone that made it function like an antenna. However, this was not true, because good coils are low loss; they do not radiate very much energy. Then I thought that the thing just acted like a base-loaded whip. This turned out to be untrue as well.

In spite of the fact that nobody really knows how these antennas work, they became the standard antenna for use on handheld transceivers during the following years. It is rumored it was Caroline Kennedy who gave the antenna its final name. She pointed to the flexible antenna on the top of a Secret Service agent's transceiver and exclaimed, "Rubber Ducky!" The name stuck.

I really did turn out to be a privileged character. I would get up in the morning with the other boys in the dormitory and go to the cafeteria with them, and then I would walk away and go to school. After school, I would stop by the TV shop and work for a few hours. Then I would walk back to Lyman and stay in my private office until bedtime. On the weekends, I would spend the entire time away. I spent the weekends working at the TV shop and sleeping at the Aldens' home.

21

The Summer Camp

The first few weeks after Westborough High School was out, I spent my time hanging around Reverend Brown's office and working on weekends at the TV shop.

Word came that a couple of other boys and I were going to summer camp. Reverend Brown asked me what I thought of that. I wanted to know more about the camp, as I had heard many bad stories about camps.

I was at a 4-H camp once, and I had not had a very good time. In fact, the person who was in charge of that camp, Skip Marshall, was always trying to prevent campers, especially me, from having a good time. Of course, I have recently learned that the camp is now called Camp Marshall, named after my nemesis. The same as for Mr. Leach—the people who gave me the hardest time are now famous and have institutions or buildings named after them. Go figure! Maybe I had a premonition that things were not going to go as well as planned. Something bothered me about going to camp. I did not quite know what it was. Perhaps the new environment was what seemed strange. I will never know.

The camp was the Charles Hayden Memorial Village in South Athol. The camp was supported by Goodwill Industries and was run by Reverend Helms. Doctor Emil Hartl and his son ran the Hayden Village, a small portion of the larger camp. As a Morgan Memorial institution, the camp was affiliated with the Charles Hayden Goodwill Inn in Boston. Doctor Hartl was well-known for his collaboration with Doctor William Sheldon, who conducted studies in child development and had established theories about a person's physical attributes relating to personality and emotional development. At the time, I just figured the place was run by some pretty smart people as well as a minister, so I told Reverend Brown, "I guess it's okay with me."

When I arrived, the camp had seven cabins at the edge of the woods overlooking a wooden bell tower. The camp also had a modern cafeteria, an auditorium, and an old building called the "Nature House." Instead of "Masters" there were "counselors." The camp equivalent of a houseboy was a counselor in training (CIT). The bell tower became the primary means of scheduling the boys' time. At six bells, we would get out of bed. At seven bells, we would go to the cafeteria for breakfast; at ten bells we would all assemble on the "rock" to be assigned our morning tasks, and on it went through the day. The camp seemed reasonable. We worked in the morning and played all afternoon.

The work assignments involved mowing the lawn with mechanical reel mowers just as at Lyman School. We also mowed the softball field, which was a major undertaking, cleaned the cabins, and washed clothes. Some boys were assigned to the cafeteria to prepare meals. Generally, the work details were created so that all the major work would be finished before lunchtime.

I did not spend much time with the other boys. I spent most of my time reading electronics magazines. This was the time that I discovered that my television invention was not an invention at all. I was surprised, but not too disappointed. Sometimes I played softball in the afternoon. At the Nature House, we had a raccoon, a bird, and a flying squirrel. The flying squirrel would climb into my shirt pocket and sleep as I read my magazines.

About a mile from the camp was a dump that the local Morgan Memorial Store used to dispose of junk that could not be sold. I spent a lot of time retrieving treasures from that dump. These treasures came in the form of old radios that I would strip for parts to fix other old radios. Soon I had a collection of over one hundred radio and television tubes. I kept these treasures and my Lyman School trombone under my bunk in the cabin.

After lunch, we would all climb into the back of a truck to take a ride to the swimming area on Spectacle Pond. The Hayden Village was not on a lake or pond, so we needed to ride a few miles to the swimming hole.

I had had very little exposure to swimming. As a small child, I never went swimming. At the pond I did not want anybody to know that I did not know how to swim, so I just thrashed around in shallow water, until one time I noticed that an empty rowboat had drifted out past the swimming area beyond the docks. I started to paddle towards the boat and noticed that it was not getting any closer. I started to feel some fear that I might not be able to get to the boat before I ran out of energy and inspiration.

I began to panic, so I decided to make long strokes on my side as an improvised self-taught sidestroke. This allowed me to keep part of my face out of the
water so I was able to breathe when I wanted. I paused, looked towards the boat,
and noticed that it was truly getting closer. I then moved to my other side and
sidestroked for a while in that new position. I continued in this way until I got to
the boat. It seemed that it took a long time to reach the boat, but when I climbed
over the transom, I discovered that I was now in the middle of the pond! I had
been swimming for perhaps as long as ten minutes!

One of the counselors came by in another boat and handed me one of his oars.
We both paddled to the shore, canoe-style. Once we tied up the boats, he
announced that since I was such a good swimmer, I was now in charge of retrieving anything that might be drifting away. Little did he know I had come within a
few seconds of a panic-induced drowning. I did eventually build upon my newfound swimming skills and was eventually able to swim across the entire pond,
something none of the other boys even dared to try!

After swimming, we would all climb aboard the truck for the ride back to the
camp. After we returned, most of us would change clothes and play softball.

Since I was new at camp, the good softball positions had already been taken. I
wanted to be pitcher, because I had eventually worked myself up to that position
at the Lyman School, but I had to start out in right field just like any newcomer.
When somebody hit a grounder out to right field, I picked up the ball and threw
it into the infield. The ball hit the pitcher in the face. I suppose he did not expect
anybody to throw the ball back into the infield. I caught him off-guard.

Anyway, I eventually worked the left field and shortstop positions before
finally pitching. I thought this was pretty good advancement, since my first-ever
ball game was at Lyman School in the early spring of the previous year.

I had been at camp for almost two months when something so horrible happened I thought it would ruin the rest of my life.

22

The Third Fire

One day about five o'clock in the afternoon during a thunderstorm, a cabin burned. Most of the campers were hanging around inside the cafeteria when some people came running from all directions pointing to cabin five. Flames were coming from all the windows. Cabin Five was my cabin! The cabin burned to the ground. By the end of the day, all the  boys who had lived in cabin five had been assigned to other cabins except me. Mr. Pendleton, the chief counselor, took me aside and told me that I would have to go back to Lyman School. I learned later that the State Police Fire Marshal had threatened to close the camp for "Fire Code" violations unless the known firebug (me) was immediately removed from the premises. This Fire Marshal was the same person who had investigated the fire at Stetson.

I told Mr. Pendleton that I had nothing to do with the fire. I had not even smoked any cigarettes since I was at camp, and I had proof that I was at the cafeteria when the fire started. I also said there was a lot of thunder and lightning, so the cabin probably was struck. He said, "It doesn't make any difference. We are not accusing you of setting the fire. You just must now leave." I knew that I was being accused, not of this specific fire, but of being a potential menace to the camp. It was not fair. I told Mr. Pendleton so. His response was, "Whoever told you that life was fair? Just be thankful that you had a couple months at the camp. Many boys never even had a chance to go to camp."

Reverend Brown came and took me back to the Lyman School. It seemed that nobody from the camp even thought enough about me to defend me, nor thought enough about themselves to defend honor. They just called the cops. The cops called Lyman.

When I returned to Lyman, I again went to Oak Cottage, the discipline cottage. That first night back from the camp was a very bad night for me. Here I was, back in the worst cottage at Lyman, with no privileges, and everyone thinking I had set a fire at camp.

23

The Runaway

Too close for comfort

I thought about running away. Runaways at Lyman were punished very severely, but I was being punished for something I had not done anyway, so I thought I had nothing much to lose. If I could make it to Ware, I could go back to work for Ed Belcher. I could find a room or apartment to rent. The only problem was that I looked too young. Ware was over sixty miles away. It would be a very difficult problem for me to go all that distance without being caught.

Maybe I could make it to Skip Anderson's house. He had a nice mother, so she might not call the cops. In order to run away, I had to be able to leave the group without being missed for at least an hour. If I could get away for about an hour, I could walk off campus without being caught. I knew just about where everybody would be during the day, so I could plan my departure so I did not encounter any work details as I left. If I could get word to Reverend Brown that I needed to see him, I would disappear after I got permission to go to his office. The Cottage Master would not let me see Reverend Brown. I tried several times to get permission to go to Bob Brown's office, but the Cottage Master insisted that I had no need to see him. There had to be another way.

Maybe the infirmary is the way, I thought. That was one way to get away. Many boys tried to pretend they were sick so that they could go to the infirmary. I was sick with a cold almost all the time, and never complained, however, so maybe that would not work for me. Most of the cottages had an iron stairway that spiraled up between floors. This was going to be my way out.

At noon on Sunday, we started down those iron stairs to the locker room to get ready for lunch. I deliberately fell down the entire flight of stairs. I was not at all hurt, but I sat on the floor at the landing and started to moan. The Cottage Master ordered me to get up and, since I did not respond to his direct order, he thought I must indeed be hurt. He summoned two houseboys and told them to take me to the infirmary to be checked out.

I hobbled to the infirmary with the aid of the two houseboys. Outside the infirmary, I told one of the houseboys, whom I knew, that I was not hurt, but I had to get out of the cottage for a few hours. He said he understood. He reached into his pocket and pulled out a worn and tattered envelope. He carefully unfolded it and displayed its contents, three five-dollar bills. With a tear in his eye, he carefully folded the envelope and put it in my shirt pocket. "Be careful," he said, "and good luck." I kissed him on the forehead, paused for a few moments, and then entered the infirmary building.

The nurse checked me out and discovered that I had a few bruises from the fall. "Nothing serious," she said, "but you can stay here overnight if you want." I told her I would be okay. She remembered me from my altercation with Mr. McPherson and asked how I was doing. I told her that things were not going very well, but that she could help me if she would just let me walk back to the cottage alone.

She asked, "Where will you go?" "I don't know yet," I explained, "I just have to find out for myself." "If you run away," she said, "they will find you and you will be in a lot of trouble." "I'm in a lot of trouble now," I said. "They think I burned down a cabin at camp." The nurse always calls the cottage when she sends someone back. I wanted her to delay that phone call as long as possible and she understood what I wanted. "How much time do you need?" asked the nurse. "Whatever I can get," I said.

I left the infirmary and quickly walked to the farmyard. The farmyard is at the edge of the institution. After I passed the barn, I was no longer in sight of most of the school's buildings, so I started to run across the fields and meadows towards the shores of Lake Chauncey. Running felt good. I felt as though I were free at last! When I came to the lake, I walked towards the main highway and started to make my way towards State Route 9. I was now about two miles from Lyman School, but in the direction opposite where I wanted to go. I stood by the side of the road trying to hitch a ride.

While I was waiting, I thought about the Lyman School and the good times that I had. I also thought about my present troubles. A man stopped his car to pick me up. He asked where I was going and I said, "Worcester." Soon we passed by the main gate of Lyman School. I felt very bad about leaving the place. I really wanted to stay. As we passed by the next overpass about a half mile down the road, I suddenly realized that I did not want to go. "Stop!" I said, "Stop the car, I have to get out." The driver looked astonished, but quickly pulled over to the side of the road. I jumped out and ran towards Lyman. I had finally learned that I could not run away from my problems.

Up the back road past Mr. Kenney's house, I ran and continued to the cottage. It was now about two o'clock. I had been gone over two hours. It was visiting hours, so the Cottage Master had not missed me at all. I found out later that Mrs. Tremblay, the nurse, never did call the cottage to tell the Master that I was being sent back to the cottage. She was going to give me all the time she could. The houseboys were astonished that I had gotten so far without being caught. As I gave my friend back his money I said, "This is where my friends are; I have nowhere else to go."

It took about a week until word got around that I had returned from camp. On a Monday, about a week after I had been kicked out of camp, I was very pleasantly surprised. Oak Cottage would be my permanent cottage and I would be a houseboy, starting now. Furthermore, the Cottage Master said, "Reverend Brown wants to see you after breakfast."

Bob Brown's office

I went to Reverend Brown's office and he looked very pleased to see me. He said the Aldens had missed me and he had just arranged for me to have a weekend with them. We talked about camp and about the fire. I learned much later that Reverend Brown had made several trips to the camp in South Athol defending me before an inquiry with the State Police Fire Marshal. He also confided that the Alden family wanted me to live at their place, but since they were adopting a Korean orphan child, the agency would not allow it.

At Oak Cottage, I did not have to do any housework. I was allowed to come and go as I pleased. My trombone had been destroyed in the fire at camp, so I played the school's piano and organ instead. Oak Cottage was where the incorri-

gibles were to stay. To this end, the strictest and meanest Cottage Master imagin-
able was in charge, Mr. Jackman. He was feared by almost everybody. He wasn't
mean to me. In fact, he was the only person at any of the institutions who asked
me how or why I committed arson. I told him that I didn't and that I accidentally burned down a barn with a rocket. He wasn't surprised that the accident had
not been discovered at trial. He knew that many of his houseboys had never been
to trial. "Damn bad break!" he said.

In a few weeks, school would be starting again and, if everything worked out, I
would be going back to Westborough High in the autumn.

24

Off to Boston

One day before school started, I was summoned to Mr. Borys' office. He told me he had good news for me. The people who ran the camp in South Athol wanted me to come and live with them in Boston. The foster home in Boston was the Charles Hayden Goodwill Inn. It was in downtown Boston on Wheeler Street.

I asked him, "How could this be? They thought I burned down their cabin at camp. How is it that now they want me to live in Boston?"

Mr. Borys said, "Oh, they found the boy who burned down the cabin; somebody by the name of Billy Smith."

Who was he talking about? Billy Smith? Had he been at the camp? I do not remember seeing him, and even if I had, would I have recognized him? Did they blame him for the fire even though everybody knew it was lightning? Maybe he made a confession, trying to help me.

The Hayden Inn

Located at 47 Wheeler Street in the south end of Boston, the Hayden Inn was a four-story brick building with a large parking lot in front. The basement contained a laundry room and a duckpin bowling alley. On the first floor were the administration offices and a dayroom with a television set. The second floor contained several large rooms that used to be classrooms. There was a pool table in the corner of one of these rooms. The rest of the rooms on this floor and all the rooms on the third were used to house the boys who were resident at the Inn. The fourth floor had a gymnasium and an apartment used by the Hartls.

I was assigned a room on the third floor. I shared this room with two other boys, one black and one white. Eventually both of my roommates were black, after the white boy went into the service. At the end of the corridor on each of the floors was a larger room that was used as the counselor's quarters. The counselors were typically college students. Near my room on the third floor was another apartment occupied by the resident manager, Mr. John B. Moreland. Mr. Moreland was a large black man who spoke impeccable English. He sounded like Sydney Poitier when he spoke. The senior staff included Mr. Pendleton, also a black man, who was second in charge.

Experimental subjects

Doctor Hartl required that the boys at Hayden have their pictures taken for Doctor Sheldon's experimental studies. These pictures were taken in four views. I did not like to have pictures taken while standing naked before a camera, but it was part of the price to pay so I could stay at the Hayden Inn. As I understand it, Doctors Hartl and Sheldon's theories on child development were famous at the time. They would classify persons into three basic types, ectomorph, mesomorph, and endomorph. These types were a classification of physical attributes. From these physical classifications, one could determine the likely emotional characteristics of the person. These theories were a likely precursor to today's widely accepted personality types, types A, B, and C. The mesomorph type was normal. In any event, supposedly you could tell from the moment of birth whether or not the child was going to grow up to be normal. This was scary. Suppose your parents wanted only normal children.

What it was like

Although the Hayden Inn was an open institution in which the residents were allowed to leave the facility as they wanted, we were isolated from other residents living in the South End of Boston because we all were identifiable as institution kids. Everyone wore the same kind of clothing. We had the typical "institution" polo shirt and khaki pants, white socks and sneakers. Our haircuts were crew cuts, so just about everywhere we went, we were identifiable. Some boys were able to obtain other kinds of clothing, but that was very rare. Morgan Memorial supported the institution, so we were called "Morgie Boys." Many of the boys at Hayden had come from the Division of Child Guardianship (DCG). They were the products of broken homes. A few others came by way of the Youth Service Board (YSB), like me.

On school days, we would arise at 6:00 AM to be ready for breakfast in the cafeteria at 7:00 AM sharp. Breakfast usually consisted of cereal and toast, although on Sundays we would have bacon and eggs. We each were supplied with a school lunch consisting of two sandwiches and some kind of fruit (usually a banana). The sandwiches were usually made from cheese with mustard, or peanut butter. The peanut butter came from a five-gallon tin and it was hard and nearly tasteless. It was not very bad, though. It gave us kids something to complain about.

After school, it was mandatory that we return to the Inn by 5:00 PM or we would not have any supper. Chores consisted of helping wash the dishes or sweeping and mopping the floors. Each had his assigned tasks. My duties, as a new resident, included working in the kitchen as a dishwasher. You were free to do whatever you wanted, provided it was legal, as soon as your chores were done. Each of the boys had his own room, which he shared with either one or two roommates. The rooms were to be kept clean, and there was an inspection every Saturday morning.

"Lights out" was supposed to be 10:00 PM, but nobody ever complied. As long as you were in bed by 10:00 PM, it was considered okay. Actually, if your roommates did not complain about the lights being on, you could keep them on as long as you wanted. Each room had a door so no other rooms would be affected. One of my roommates could sleep anywhere and nothing ever bothered him. My other roommate usually kept his light on all the time. It did not bother me.

At one time, I had a roommate who absolutely could not sleep in a bed. He would get up after he thought I was asleep and lay down on the floor with only a blanket. The floor was tiled concrete and cold!

I attended Roslindale High School. In the early morning, I would take the elevated train to Forest Hills, then the Mattapan bus to Roslindale center. The principal of the school was called a "Headmaster," as was the tradition of the "English High School" system in Boston. His name was Doctor O'Leary.

The fight

During my second week at the school, a boy walked up to me during homeroom class and started to "rank" me. To rank someone was to insult his or her parentage, nationality, or other factor you had no control over in an effort to start a fight. A typical rank might be, "Your mother wears combat boots." Generally, as soon as you heard the word "mother" mentioned, you knew that the idea was to start a fight. Some ranks were quite contrived, such as, "I'll rank you so low that you'll be doing push-ups under a razor blade on a whale's balls—and that's way below sea level!" I knew that it was only a matter of time before somebody attempted to start a fight with me. That is the way the pecking order is established. The usual result with many boys was that they would back down and not get involved in a fight at all. The problem was that once you backed down, you would be the subject of ridicule for many months. I had enough problems with ridicule just being a "Morgie Boy."

I knew from the sound of his voice just where the boy was standing. I never looked up. Instantly I jumped up from my chair then to the top of my desk. I grabbed the boy around the neck and dragged him over to the window. With much effort and strain, I rolled him over the sill and out the window. He fell to the ground below. The classroom was on the second floor. Incidentally, I never even knew the boy's name.

The class was suddenly very quiet as I walked back to my seat. In a few minutes, I was summoned to the Headmaster's office and dismissed from school. When I returned to the Inn, I told Mr. Pendleton about the incident. He inquired about how the other boy was. I told him I did not know, but he was probably okay since the fall was not very far. Mr. Pendleton and Mr. Moreland talked to the Headmaster and I was allowed to return to school the following Monday; so I was out of school for only a few days.

When I returned to the class, I found that I never had to worry about being picked on again. I heard other boys talking about me: "Don't mess with him! He's *crazy*. He'll throw the bomb on you." My nickname became "The Mad Bomber." Friends called me the "Bad Momber," and I did make many friends. The boy who started the fight never returned to school. I have never had another fight in my entire life. That fight helped me develop an attitude that has kept potential assailants at bay! I had learned to stand my ground and defend myself. This was an essential benchmark of my continuing growth as a maturing child.

The elevator

The Hayden Inn had an elevator. The resident kids were not allowed to use the elevator; only the counselors and other important people were. "Why is it that I can't use the elevator?" I asked Mr. Pendleton one day. His response was, "You need an elevator operator's license to run an elevator." I could see how this must be true because the elevator operated with just a handle, and you had to very carefully slow it down at just the right rate, to get it to stop on the correct floor. Otherwise, you would have to step up or step down when getting on or off to make up for the errors. I decided to get an elevator operator's license. I made friends with an elevator operator at the Bradford Hotel across the street and learned how to operate a manual elevator properly.

Then I made an appointment at the City Hall to take the test. The day of the test, I needed two dollars to pay the fee. I could not find anyone with two dollars to borrow. I walked up to the City Hall anyway and told a clerk about my problem. "If I could just borrow two dollars to pay for the test today," I told her, "I'll bring it back as soon as my boss comes back tomorrow." A whole bunch of people in that office chipped in to pay the fee. The test involved a written portion and a practical portion. The written questions were about Boston's fire regulations, and the chief elevator operator at City Hall administered the practical portion. I passed the test fine.

When I returned to the Hayden Inn, I showed the license to Mr. Moreland. He was more proud than I ever expected. I had just become the only licensed elevator operator in the place and the only one who could legally use the elevator!

25

The Church Organ

On Wheeler Street between the Hayden Inn and the Seavey Building was an old church, the Church of All Nations. I discovered that the church contained a gigantic theater organ. This was a real pipe organ with many ranks of pipes and bells. It had been electrified, so it was only necessary to find the hidden switch to turn on the blowers and bring this magnificent monster to life. However, because of its poor condition, it was not used for church services. The first time I played the organ I was concerned that I might be discovered by somebody and kicked out. Perhaps they would lock the church doors, so I would never be able to play the instrument again. Worse, somebody would probably call the police and I would be beaten or arrested. It was for this reason that when I started
playing the organ, I would only play church hymns, so that anyone who heard the organ would think that is was the organist practicing for Sunday services.

The organ had quite a few problems. If one pulled out all the stops, it would run out of air and start to make groaning sounds. The natural chuff that begins each note would turn into a squeal. If I tried to play the organ loudly, it would begin to sound like a circus calliope. Many of the keys would stick, so it was not very easy to play. I decided that I would fix that organ. Dr. Hartl was associated with the Church of All Nations and he told me that as long as it didn't cost anything I could try to fix the organ.

The first thing I did was go to the library. I went to the Boston Public Library and got a library card. When I put down my address as 27 Wheeler Street, the library clerk said that she would give me a card, but I could not take out any books. I asked her why. She said, "You Morgie Boys never return the books." I asked her why I should even get a library card if I could not take out books.

She responded with, "Then I won't let you into the library!" I said, "Anybody can come into the library, it's a public library!" She said, "Not you!"

This was just an indication of what was to come. Practically every time there was poor weather, or I found I did not have anything else to do, I would walk over to the library and hang around, reading books. I thought the purpose of the library was to have a place to hang around. I did not know that it was illegal. Anyway, after the library clerk would see me at a reading table several days in a row, she would threaten to call the police and have me arrested. I asked my homeroom teacher at Roslindale High if somebody could do that. She said, "Of course not! The Boston Public Library is a public place. It is even famous. Unless you are disruptive, nobody can kick you out!" She did not know how wrong she was!

The next time the library clerk told me to go. I told her no. I said, "Leave me alone. I am not doing anything wrong. You can't force me to leave." Well, I did not know anything about it. It seems that library clerks are called librarians and they have great power, probably passed down from the same people who made the Stubborn Child laws. I wish I were kidding. Boston had an ordinance that gave librarians considerable power. They could solely determine if some person within the library was a disreputable person and was, therefore, out of order. They could force one to leave by such a determination. She called the police and two police officers came and walked me out of the library. I had become a disreputable person.

One cop said, "The next time the librarian tells you to leave, you better fuckin' leave. I'm gonna let you get away with your fuckin' sassy attitude just once. The next time, I'll fuckin' run you in."

In Boston police lingo, "run you in" meant "I'll beat the hell out of you!" The police did not generally take you to court for things like this. They would just beat you.

I felt lucky. They did not beat me up. The library had an outdoor area where one could take books without having to check them out. As soon as the clerk discovered that I was using the outdoor area, she grabbed me and threatened to call the cops again. So, I was forced to spend any time at the library in the big reading room in front of that creepy clerk. I learned a lot while reading old books in the library. I even learned how to repair the organ.

I spent much of my free time learning about the construction and operation of theater organs. I learned about the way the keys operate the air valves, the way the air pressure was supposed to be regulated (which was not working in the organ I was playing), and how to tune the pipes. I really wanted to fix that organ, but I did not have any money to buy leather to repair the air chest, which had been wired shut because the old leather was broken. This was the reason why the organ could not be played loudly. What I needed was a sponsor. I would do the work, but somebody else had to buy the materials. While I was waiting to find a sponsor, I repaired the sticking keys with sandpaper and paste wax, which I could afford to purchase.

On Saturday afternoon, I would go to the library and wait around the loft where the organ books were stored. Finally, I found someone who was reading about old theater organs. He was an old man, probably in his sixties, who was very interested in organs. I approached him. "I've been trying to repair an old organ in the church, but I don't have the money to buy leather," I said. "Would you like to see the organ and maybe help me buy some stuff to fix it?" The old man just looked past me, turned abruptly, and walked away. I guessed that I would have to find another way to repair the organ. Maybe I could just steal the leather. I also needed some real horsehide glue, and I did not know where I would get that. It has to be heated up, so I would need a glue pot as well. Maybe I would have to wait for another person who was interested in organs to show up at the library.

The next week the old man walked up to me in the library and asked, "So you're trying to fix up an old organ, eh?"

"Yes," was my response, "the organ's in the church across the street from where I live, and I want to fix it up."

"Why would you want to work on an organ that's not yours? It's not yours, is it?"

"No," I said, "but they don't play it on Sunday in the church because it doesn't work right. They play the piano instead. I want to fix up the organ so I can play it. I've already got it to play pretty well since I fixed all the stuck keys."

The old man interrupted me: "Come on, let's go see your organ."

The man's name was Mr. Volker. He lived in South Boston. He was a music teacher and piano tuner. He had a small store where he sold sheet music and gave piano lessons. We went to the church and he played the organ. The organ did not sound very good, but Mr. Volker really knew how to play that organ. After Mr. Volker looked over the inner workings of the organ he said, "I'll make you a deal. I will get you the leather and equipment you need. However, you are going to have to do all the work. I'm an old man, now, and I can't be crawling around inside this thing." I was elated! I had found a friend who would sponsor me. I took him across the street to the Hayden Inn and showed him around. I even showed him my "Ham Radio" station in the basement. He was quite surprised that I had so many interests. "Tomorrow," said Mr. Volker, "you come to my store. We'll get started right away."

Over the next month, I worked entire weekends on that organ, always with Mr. Volker at my side. We repaired the air chest and set up the pressure on the blower. We replaced rubber hoses that were so old that they had become like hard plastic. Mr. Volker showed me how to balance the keys, so that a light pressure would cause a soft sound and a heavy pressure would make them sound loud. We reconnected ranks of pipes that had been disconnected over the years. Eventually we got it working so well that it was time to tune it.

You tune a pipe organ by first getting one set of pipes (the flutes) to sound on key. You do this by setting up the middle octave by "ear" and then sounding each successive octave and bending lead tuners on the pipes to get them to sound in synchronism. After this, you tune the other pipes into resonance with the first. This takes many hours of hard work climbing up around the pipes and tuning them. As each set of pipes was tuned, they would detune the previous ones, so it was necessary to restart repeatedly. Eventually after several days of work, we got all the major pipes to sound together. The very low woods and the clappers could not be tuned because they had been mistuned by someone whittling away wood from the throats. Mr. Volker brought some teak wood and we rebuilt many of the wooden pipes.

It took about three weekends just to tune the organ, but it was worth it! The organ really sounded great. Mr. Volker played Edward Elgar's *Pomp and Circumstance*. It was so great that I was embarrassed to try to play anything after that. "No," said Mr. Volker, "it is now your time to play your organ. I have heard you play. You play very well. Now you play." About the only piece that I knew how to play well enough to dare play it for Mr. Volker was Dvořák's *Humoresque*. I had attempted to play it on this organ before it was repaired, so I guessed I had nothing to lose. Slowly I started to play. As I continued, my fingers started to become part of the keys. My heart ran out through my fingertips and into this great grand organ. My feet danced on the pedals. I had become part of the organ.

It was a great feeling. Mr. Volker reached over my shoulder and opened another stop. The organ came to life. I played on past the end of the piece. I added my own variations as I had done with the Hammond organ at Lyman. I was so very happy.

I looked up at Mr. Volker and he had tears running down his cheeks. "You come to my store," said Mr. Volker, "and I'll teach you everything I know. You will be a great musician."

About once a week, I did go by Mr. Volker's store. He would give me some sheet music to practice. Sometimes I would ride the subway with him when he would go out to tune somebody's piano. One Saturday morning in December, I was playing a piece on the church organ and I heard a noise behind me. I was quite used to hearing noises since many people were now coming to the church to hear me play. At times, people would come up to the loft and talk to me. I even met a woman who wanted me to play at her daughter's wedding. This time it was different. I heard the sound of heavy keys on a belt. I could hear the squeaking of leather. I turned from my perch on the organ bench just in time to see an enormous police officer swing his club at my head. "What the fuck you think you're doing?" he bellowed, as he swung the baton.

I covered my head and face, jumped from the bench, and cowered in the corner. A painful flurry of flying feet and swinging clubs followed. I screamed. From off in the distance I heard a man yell, "Unhand that boy!" I did not hear anything more.

Soon I felt cold. I looked around and I found myself lying outside the church in falling snow. I had no jacket and was in great pain. I slowly walked, almost crawling, to the Hayden Inn and went inside. I made my way to my room and looked into the mirror. Blood covered my face and head. Damn, I thought, I am really messed up. Over several weeks, my wounds healed. My roommate thought I must have been in a fight. My right hand was broken, I had deep gashes in the top of my head, and my nose bled for several days. Mr. Moreland, the resident manager, playfully asked, "How's the other kid look?" You see, it was normal for kids who lived at the Hayden Inn to be beaten up.

I never played the organ again.

26

Looking for a Job

I spent much of my free time exploring industrial junkyards for electronic components. I found where
Western Electric was disposing of
their old telephone equipment.
Eventually I set up an entire dial telephone exchange in my room. When
my room got so crowded with electronic equipment that my roommates were unable to enter, Mr.
Pendleton found me a storage room
to use as a laboratory in the basement. I installed my amateur radio
antenna on the roof and operated my
six-meter station from the basement.
I was not a very good student in high
school, but I kept out of trouble and
kept very busy with my electronics
hobby, so I was no problem to
anyone.

I tried to get a job at a TV repair
shop, but the owners would refuse to believe that I knew anything about electronics. Everywhere I would turn, I would find that somebody thought that I was
just some stupid Morgie Boy who had more nerve than brains. I decided that I
had to get an FCC license to show the nonbelievers that I knew what I was doing.
At the time, a third class license allowed you only to talk on a radio. The second
class allowed you to repair FCC-licensed radio transmitters, and the first class was
the PhD of licenses, which allowed you to work at radio and television stations.

I set out to get the second class license. My first stop at the Custom House in Boston got me the third class license, which was next to worthless, but a necessary step towards the second and first class ones. The second class license was much harder to obtain. I failed the test several times, but I would just wait another sixty days, the required waiting period, and then skip school to take the test again. Finally, I obtained the second class radio license.

Before the ink was dry, I tried just about every TV repair shop from Roslindale to Lynn to find a part-time job. I was never able to obtain one. I found a job listing at a fire station where they wanted someone to maintain the department's two-way radios. My FCC license, as well as my experience with police radios, qualified me for that job, but the supervisor took my license away when I went to apply, claiming that I must have stolen it. I called the local FCC office at the Custom House and the engineer in charge of the Radio District said that he would watch for it if it were turned in. He received it and sent it back to me. His name was Nathan Hallenstein.

Mr. Pendleton had arranged for the boys from the Hayden Inn to attend a movie theater, just down Tremont Street from the Inn, at a reduced rate. One Saturday afternoon, I peeked into the projection booth and watched the projectionist at work. At first the projectionist told me to go away. I told him that I was working on getting my first class radio operator's license, I had just obtained my second class license, and I was very interested in his job, because someday I expected to work at television stations. He invited me into the booth and showed me the equipment. The equipment was a Westar projector, which used Peerless Magnarc carbon arcs to produce the light, and a Western Electric Westrex sound head. A large audio rack contained vacuum tube amplifiers to drive the speakers, and some vacuum tube regulators for the projector. This was all quite impressive, much like the radio station up on the hill in Paxton. The projectionist's name was Mr. Crawford. He told me that if I got my apprentice projectionist's license he would teach me what I needed to know to obtain my journeyman's projectionist license.

It turns out that the apprentice projectionist license involved taking a test about local fire regulations, much the same test that I had taken for my elevator operator's license. I needed to get this slip of paper so that my mentor could log the hours of "instruction" that I had obtained so I would qualify to take the journeyman's license test. In principle, I had to log one thousand hours of instruction, which really meant that I had had to work full-time, about half a year, without pay. Although this seemed impossible, I took the apprentice test anyway.

This allowed me to work in the projection booth, when I was available, in exchange for seeing the movie.

In about four months, Mr. Crawford had to leave to move to another city. I asked him about the license. He said that he would sign me off to take the test and, if I passed the test, he would recommend me for his job. I was going to high school full time so I could not take a full-time job, but I took the test anyway. It cost ten dollars to take that test, after which I became a journeyman projectionist with only a few actual hours of actual instruction. That was illegal, immoral, and fattening. Do not tell anybody, all right?

One special kind of job

Many of the boys at Hayden were able to purchase nice clothing from their part-time jobs. Since I did not have a job, I continued to wear the institution's clothing, which marked me as a loser. "How is it," I asked my roommate, "that you have a part-time job that makes you lots of money, but I can't even get a job sweeping floors?" My roommate responded, "I just go out hustlin'. I get all the money I need."

"What on earth is hustling?" I asked. My roommate thought I must be very naïve, or very stupid, so he refused to tell me what it meant. I asked someone else.

"You just go out to the Commons or Gardens," I was told. "Just sit on the benches. Pretty soon somebody comes by and sits down beside you. He'll ask if you want to fool around or something. You never have to do anything. You just go with him and he'll give you five dollars. Sometimes you get even fifteen or twenty dollars. Sometimes you get the same guy as before. He treats you special and buys you some new clothes or something. He's called a sugar daddy." This seemed to me to be the worst way in the world to make money.

Another told me that there was a system. You sit on the third step up on the right at the Park Street Church between three and four o'clock on Saturday afternoon. A priest will come by and ask you about the Red Sox. This is your cue. He really wants to know if you want to make some money going with him. The stated fee schedule seemed to correlate with the other information I had received.

I could not imagine how my friends and roommates could ever do such things. "That's what fags are for!" was the explanation.

I figured that if I really got hard up for money I could do this stuff, but since all I wanted was a good shirt and some decent pants, I felt I was not that bad off yet. Instead, I had a telephone-booth route. I would take the transmitter out of the mouthpieces of several telephones near South Station. Every day, I would go back and put in a transmitter before hanging up the receiver. I would be rewarded with the money that the telephone company customers had lost, trying to make a call. Some machines paid quite well!

Eventually I got a part-time job that earned me a little money. I helped mow the lawn at Forest Hills Cemetery. This was interesting: by that time, I had a FCC second class radiotelephone license, which qualified me to repair FCC-licensed radio equipment such as police car radios; I also had an elevator operator's license, a journeyman's projectionist's license, and a driver's license. However, to earn spending money, I had to mow cemetery lawns at minimum wage. Go figure!

27

The Sweaters

The first sweater

A friend of mine, about one year younger than me, had his
sweater stolen while at school. He was very distraught,
since it had been a very nice sweater given to him by a
sugar daddy. He used to wear that sweater all the time and
now he practically looked naked without it. He said he
would have to go out to the park and see if he could get
some more money to buy another one. I told him to wait.
I did not want him to go out to the park and sell his body. I would get him
another sweater. I went to a large department store on North Washington Street,
picked out a sweater for him, then just walked out the front door without even
looking back! To me, this was not really stealing. I was just equalizing the wealth.
I guess you could say it was being like Robin Hood. My friend was very happy
with the new sweater and we became very close.

And the second sweater

One of my roommates had a similar sweater, except his
sister had given it to him. He, too, would wear the sweater
all the time, sometimes even to bed. It was quite worn and
he had attempted to sew it together in several places. At
one time, it had had a reindeer pattern. Now it was so
faded that the reindeer looked somewhat like white rats.
    One day my roommate came home from school carry-
ing his sweater in a lunch bag. Some school kids had ripped it off his back and set
it on fire. Schoolchildren can be very cruel. He was very distraught, about as close
to crying as a fifteen-year-old would allow.
    Anyway, I told him not to worry. I ran off and did my Robin Hood trick
again. When I returned with a brand-new sweater, he burst into a rage, threw it

into the corridor, and claimed that I did not have a clue. It was several years later that I started to understand. It was true: I really did not have a clue at the time. Eventually I learned there is a difference between a sweater you get from your sister, and a sweater you get from being a whore. Go figure! Nevertheless, I liked playing Robin Hood on occasion and I was never caught in the act!

28

The NAACP and Black Culture

Mr. Pendleton was involved in some of the early civil rights work, and Mr. Moreland was interested in jazz. The NAACP held Sunday afternoon meetings in a Roxbury church where they showed films taken on southern civil rights trips. Afterwards they would march up Washington Street to the Boston Common where they  would hold a rally. The Boston Police Department did not like the fact that the NAACP was showing films that displayed the southern police beating people, so they declared that no films could be shown unless a licensed projectionist showed them. They cited some "Fire Code" law that stated that if more than three persons were viewing a film, a licensed projectionist needed to be running the projector. The police apparently thought that the local chapter would never be able to find a licensed projectionist to show the films. Mr. Pendleton got me a job running the projector because I had the required license. The projector was on loan from the Hayden Inn as well, because the police had confiscated the NAACP's projector. Think about this for a moment. The police confiscated a projector because movies of real happenings were showing in a church.

Every Sunday afternoon I would take the MTA to Roxbury, while carrying the projector, which was almost as large as I was. After the film, I would often join the march and walk all the way back to Boston with the group. It never bothered me that I was the only white person in the group. One time I shook the hand of Doctor Martin Luther King. It was like shaking the hand of God himself.

One of the NAACP members asked me what color I thought God's skin was. This was supposed to be some kind of a cruel joke and I was about to be the target since I was a white boy. I could not think of anything funny to say. Instead, I responded, "God's skin is the color of love." I had not planned to say anything like that; the words just rolled, uncontrolled, from my lips. People who heard me were suddenly stunned into silence. One black minister told me I had the "calling." I should become a minister myself.

John Moreland, called J. B. for short, organized trips for some of us boys. He would sometimes sneak a few of us onto the rooftop at the Bradford Hotel when special jazz bands were playing. One time he took four of us boys to the Green Hill Country Club near Worcester. Duke Ellington was playing. Both Duke Ellington and Billie Holliday met us at our table. J. B. introduced us in turn. When Billie asked what I was drinking, I said that I was drinking Coca Cola. She said, "Try this," and offered me a sip from her glass. It was a Singapore Sling, and I can claim that my lips touched the glass that touched the lips of Billie Holliday.

Eventually J. B. got a few jiggers of rum to sweeten our cokes. Before the night was over, we had all been introduced to one of the greatest experiences one could imagine. Also, on the following morning, we had one of the worst hangovers!

Most of the boys at the Hayden Inn were black. In fact, there was not too much emphasis upon race at Hayden. We were all together, with a common enemy: "You and me against the world!" The world was rich. We were poor. We dedicated a lot of effort to becoming unpoor. This was the culture taught by J. B. Moreland. Mr. Pendleton announced that the NAACP should really be called the NAAPP, National Association for the Advancement of Poor People; being black was all about being poor, nothing else. Furthermore, the NAACP was founded by a multiracial group who knew about being poor.

There was no such thing as black English among us. All the boys at the Hayden Inn attempted to emulate Mr. Moreland with his impeccable British English. Black boys at Roslindale High also sounded just like the white boys. Of course, we all knew some street slang that we would use to advantage if the occasion required. I guess one might call that "rap" nowadays. The following, pronounced in an exaggerated southern twang, "Don' you be callin' me no mo' fucker—mo' fucker this an' mo' fucker that—I'll kick you ass an' stomp you hat!" might be the proper response if somebody insulted you, but of course you might have to back that up with some action.

One time Mr. Pendleton went to visit his mother in Philadelphia. It was in the summertime and we were at camp in South Athol. He asked Ray Smith, one of my roommates, and me if we would like to take the automobile trip to Philadelphia with him. Of course, we wanted to go. Once we were in Philadelphia, Mr. Pendleton said we needed to take the train to Baltimore because his sick mother had been transferred to a hospital there. I was dumbfounded that Baltimore had colored waiting rooms in the train stations and colored men's rooms in the subways. Incidentally, they seemed to have fixed the racial equality problem later on by getting rid of all the men's rooms altogether.

Mr. Moreland taught us the culture of working hard and playing hard. Any time spent idle was a waste of one's life. We did not just hang around like many of my classmates. Instead, we were always doing something and, one would hope, staying out of trouble at the same time. With the Civil Rights activists starting to be noticed by the media, there was an increased awareness of race, even in Boston, which was quite civilized, and by national standards, quite liberal at the time. A reporter came to Hayden Inn, and when she was being shown around, she asked why I shared a room with two black boys. One of my roommates interrupted with a joke in street slang, "It's okay. He's our token honky!"

29

The Boston Science Fair

At school, I spent a lot of my time working on a science fair project. The science teacher, himself an amateur radio operator, had taken a liking to me, and I was allowed unlimited access to the physics laboratory. I decided to make a rate gyroscope for my project. It was to emulate a laser ring gyro. My science teacher only expected me to display and diagram the components of a laser gyroscope. I decided to actually make one.

Massachusetts
Science Fair

My first laser ring gyro did not use a laser because, although we had heard of lasers with their ruby crystals and xenon flash tubes, they were quite a bit beyond the league of high school students. Instead, my ring gyroscope used sound. It was, therefore, an acoustic ring gyro. Both acoustic and laser gyroscopes work on the same inertial principles. Further, because of government secrecy, the typical high school student, me included, didn't know that one needed to use a special laser that was quite different from the ruby lasers being disclosed in scientific publications.

My acoustic ring gyro consisted of a roll of plastic tubing about fifty feet in length and about one-quarter inch inside diameter. This roll of tubing was left on its spool, just as purchased, so that, as sound propagated through, it would go around and around the axis of the spool.

I used piezoelectric earphone transducers that you could purchase for portable radios for both the transmitter and receiver. One was coupled to the starting end of the roll of tubing, and the other coupled to its finish.

In those days, you could buy transistors (Raytheon CK-722), but they were very expensive and very fragile, so all the electronics I built used vacuum tubes. I made a Wien bridge audio oscillator with an amplified output that fed one of the transducers. It generated a sine wave at a frequency that was found to propagate through the tubing with minimum loss. The frequency was about three kilohertz. I also made a vacuum-tube amplifier to amplify the signal captured by the other transducer. The two signals, the original fed into the tubing, and the received signal that had traveled the length of the tubing in the circuitous path, were fed to a phase detector that used two pairs of diodes (6AL5 tubes). A balanced DC amplifier using a 12AX7 vacuum tube amplified the output.

There were various potentiometers used to adjust a center-scale milliammeter to zero when everything was balanced. Now, if you changed the plane of rotation of these sound waves, the phase between the input and output would change. This was, therefore, a rate gyro, similar to the turn needle, a primitive turn coordinator, on an aircraft panel, except that it was electronic, had no moving mechanical parts, and was so sensitive that it could detect the rotation of the earth.

During experimentation, I found that if I zeroed the meter with the coil of tubing lying in one direction, it would no longer be zeroed when lying on its other side. This difference was caused by the rotation of the earth. In fact, I was able to find the neutral plane, where zeroing it with it rotating in one direction would also result in a null in the other direction. This corresponded exactly to the latitude of Boston, near where I performed my experiments.

As sensitive as it was, it did have a shortcoming that I quickly discovered. The velocity of sound, and therefore the sensitivity of this acoustic gyro, is greatly dependent upon temperature. To make a practical device, one would have to use two rolls of tubing to make a "counter-rotating" acoustic gyro, or two gyros in which the difference was produced as output, rather than the individual value. Of course, the ideal device would have sound traveling in both directions in the same roll of tubing. I did not know how to do that. In one fell swoop, I invented a method of compensating for the temperature effects of something that no one had even thought of yet, the fiber-optic gyro.

Early laser gyros, called strap-down gyros, were expensive, and used a laser beam reflected around and around a prism. The laser gyro used a beam splitter to make two counter-rotating beams, plus an additional splitter, used in reverse as a combiner. The combined beams were detected in an interferometer. This was all very critical and complicated stuff. Once somebody made fiber-optic cables and laser diodes, thirty years after my invention, the laser gyro became trivial. Just replace my acoustic tubes with optical fiber, and you are done.

My high school physics teacher was very impressed. He was sure that I had created a great invention, and now he tried to get me discovered. When he approached Sperry Gyroscope, they arranged for a trip to their facility on Long Island. He thought that Sperry might give me a scholarship or offer me a job, or both. This was before they became Sperry Rand. It was an exciting trip taking the train from Boston, so it was not a complete waste of time. I showed a number of people, some wearing suits (maybe lawyers), and some wearing slacks (maybe engineers) the workings of my gyro.

They all seemed impressed. They brought us to a fancy restaurant and then sent us on our way. Two days later, I received a telegram. I had never received a telegram before in my life! The telegram was a Cease and Desist Order from the Federal District Court in Islip, New York, requiring that any work on this device be immediately suspended. A follow-up was a hand-delivered court order requiring that any materials or documents relating to this device be surrendered. My physics teacher took care of the details. Everything I had been working on was tagged by two federal agents, put into a large cardboard container marked "evidence," and taken away.

I guess I had stumbled upon the inner workings for some ICBM guidance system and they, whoever they were, did not want me to disclose how easily an electronic gyroscope could be made. Either that, or the researchers at Sperry were just a bunch of crooks, claiming that they invented something that I had invented.

My high school science fair project was now gone.

Now I had to complete another science fair project in only two weeks. I decided to build an antenna and prove its design. Since I already had a six-meter transmitter and receiver that I had built, this antenna would be very useful for my radio station. In addition, I would be able to complete all the design necessary to make a commercial antenna. I would predict and measure antenna power gain, directivity, matching characteristics, and all the other stuff necessary to produce a commercial electronic product.

During this project, I carefully calculated the length of each of the antenna elements, carefully assembled and tested the antenna, and then prepared much documentation verifying the design. I prepared posters demonstrating the methods used to measure the antenna characteristics. I even produced a graphical analysis in experimental proof of Huygens' Principle (a highly theoretical basis for antenna design analysis).

I won a prize in the Boston competition, so this made me eligible to compete in the statewide competition being held in Westborough.

The winners are...

The winner of the science fair was a lad who hooked up a couple of light bulbs to a telephone dial and called it a digital computer. I think he was related to the Headmaster of the English High School system. The runner-up was his sister with her butterfly collection. I was beginning to learn about politics.

I was so furious that I tore everything up and smashed the antenna to bits. Repeatedly I kept slamming it into the wall until I was completely exhausted. Then I sat down and cried.

I overheard someone say, "You know, it happens every year. They get these kids whipped up into a frenzy, preparing for the science fair, then the judges come in and blow everybody outa the water with their favoritism. If I were that kid, I'd shoot the judges." Well, I did not shoot the judges, but when I realized there were so many people who felt just like me, it made the whole thing worth it. Little did they know that I had already been screwed by a federal judge in New York on the science fair project of the century. These science fair judges meant nothing in comparison. Maybe someday there will be a real science fair, I thought.

My science teacher carefully picked up the pieces and put them in the trunk of his car. At another time, I would repair the antenna and use it with my ham station.

30

Back to Camp

When school was out for the summer, we went back to the camp at South Athol. I was now seventeen years of age. I was a CIT, which allowed me a few extra privileges. I set up my amateur radio station in the carpentry shop behind the place where cabin five had burned. During the previous summer, I had spent many hours talking on the radio to hams all around the state. Several

even came to see me at the camp. I had a good time at camp. I was involved in all kinds of activities including amateur theater at the playhouse.

My playacting career started when I became the playhouse electrician and ran the lights. I even installed a new set of footlights at the open-air theater in South Athol Center. I also got to play the Vicar in *See How They Run*. It was a very good experience for me, and I enjoyed it very much.

The counselor who ran the Nature House would let me drive his car when we would go into town on errands. When I was ready, he let me drive to Holyoke, Massachusetts, to take the driver's test. I got my driver's license while at camp that summer. My parents even came to visit me once while I was at camp.

While at camp, I built an electronic kit for Dr. Hartl. The kit was an EICO stereo tuner. I built it with the utmost of care, and it worked the very first time it was turned on. He gave me a carton of cigarettes for my work. I also built and installed an intercom system so that music could be played from a central receiver and fed to all of the cabins. The front end of the system was installed in the rear of the cafeteria and from there it was possible to page anyone at any of the cabins.

I wired up all the cabins with wire I had obtained from abandoned telephone circuits that used to run through the woods.

One of the counselors took me aside one day and asked me to watch several boys who were suspected of homosexual activities. I was to report to him if I saw anything that would confirm some information previously received from some other sources. The counselor knew that I was just about the most trusted person at camp. The rest of the kids trusted me, as did the counselors themselves. I was being asked to betray this trust. My own ideas about sexuality were that having sex with your friend was for having fun and having sex with a girl was for making babies. I never equated homosexuality with either of these things. Homosexuality, to me, was like the people in the park paying some kid for sex, or like when I had been raped at Stetson and the YSB. The first thing I did was go straight to the boys who were being suspected and told them they were being watched, so they should be very careful. I never said, "Do this," or "Don't do this." I just told them that so-and-so had it in for them, so they should be very careful. To this day, I consider myself a very lucky person to have never been taught to be prejudiced or bigoted. I had learned firsthand that it was very important to be loved. Everything else was secondary. The boys loved me for my advice.

This counselor was quite obviously an untrustworthy person with a serious mental problem, who was trying to make trouble. He continued to make trouble at the Hayden Inn, but we were onto him and stayed well clear. He would sneak down the corridor when the boys were in their rooms at night, then suddenly yank open the door and switch on the light, trying to catch somebody doing something wrong. My roommates and I rigged up our door so that a water-filled balloon fell on his head when he did that to us. The water therapy worked. He stayed away from our room after that.

31

Home Again the Final Time

After camp was over, I told Mr. Pendleton that I wanted to go out on my own. "I've got a second class FCC license, which will get me a job in any city. I've got an automobile license, and I know how to take care of myself," I said.

"Yes," said Mr. Pendleton, "but you haven't finished school!"

I told him I would never be able to finish school here. I inquired, "If I can't go out on my own, maybe I could go back home with my parents?"

Mr. Pendleton told me that since I was now over sixteen, the law no longer required that I attend school. "But it'd be such a waste for you to quit," he said.

Belchertown

"Well, I won't quit if I can go home to my folks," was my response. I had not realized that the Hayden Inn had been doing much more than providing me with a place to eat and sleep. They had been protecting me from the police. I will tell more about that in a moment.

So this was how I came to move back home. I agreed to continue school if they agreed to let me go home. My father came and brought me to his new home in Belchertown. I was soon to learn that there were no provisions made by my folks for me to continue school anyway. "Now you're home. Now you work!" was my mother's response. I was required to pay twenty-five dollars per week for my room and board. I went to work at Ware Radio Service for a short time, sharing a ride with another technician who lived in Belchertown. In about four months, I quit and took a job at the Television Center in Amherst, servicing tele-

126

vision sets. My pay was about seventy-five dollars per week. Soon I rented a room and moved away from home forever. I was eighteen years of age.

I was not quite completely free, yet. As an emancipated juvenile, one who was supporting himself and living on his own, I was supposed to have the same rights as an adult. This was not, in fact, what was happening. I do not know how the state police had learned that I moved from Boston. I suppose the police did not dare pick on the youngsters while they were living at the Hayden Inn because of the strong influence of Mr. Moreland, Mr. Pendleton, and Doctor Hartl. When I started living on my own that protection was no longer available.

Even obtaining an automobile was very difficult. I purchased my 1954 Chevy for $350 cash from a dealer in Amherst. I paid over $500 cash for insurance. The local registry of motor vehicles in Holyoke refused to let me register it, so I had to take a bus to Boston and wait in line for several days as the officials threw about every possible obstacle in my path. I was told that known delinquents were not allowed to own or register motor vehicles in the state of Massachusetts. I looked up all the Massachusetts Motor Vehicle Laws at the Boston Public Library, and there wasn't any mention at all about delinquents, whether known or not.

Mr. Rudolph King was the man in charge of the Massachusetts Motor Vehicle Department; I walked right into his office and asked him to tell his people to give me a registration.

He picked up his telephone and it was done.

Practically every time there was a fire anywhere in the state, I was picked up and questioned for as much as twelve hours. In the first year of living on my own, I took polygraph tests five times at the State Police barracks in Northampton.

My last polygraph session was most memorable. Maybe you can figure out why anybody bothers to perform polygraph examinations. The polygraph examiner made a list of questions that could be answered yes or no. As I recall, there were about ten questions. We went over the questions and answers ahead of time without the machine running, then he turned on the machine and we ran through the questions while I answered each one in turn.

After the ten questions, he asked, "Are you afraid that I might ask more questions?" I answered that question and then he stated, "You can be assured that I won't ask any more questions than the ones we rehearsed." The cycle repeated, and he asked all the questions again. After he ran through the questions twice, I asked him if he was aware that he had just asked me eleven questions, the ones we wrote down in the beginning, and the one that he asked me about being afraid of more questions.

He said, "Yes, that's how we know if you are telling the truth. You see, I teach you what truth is. That's how the polygraph works."

"Okay," I said, "since we both know what truth is, please tell the State Police Fire Marshal to get off my back!" He said he would.

One of the questions had been, "Are you fascinated by fire?" The polygraph examiner was surprised that I answered it with "yes," although I had no particular fascination with fire. After the polygraph examination, he asked me to explain that answer, which seemed to indicate that I was not telling the truth. I told him that I may not actually be fascinated by fire, but I was sure the Fire Marshal was. That is why he got into his line or work. The same may be true for volunteer firemen. They are likely all fascinated by fire. This fascination does not mean that they set fires. It is just an underlying incentive to work with fire, so the question in the polygraph test was not a good question to use if you want to discover if somebody set a fire.

"The correct question," I said, "is 'Did you set the fire?' and, by the way, you never even asked me that!" He said he did not have to. He knew the fire was not set. I told him that my juvenile arson conviction had nothing to do with setting a fire. I burned down a barn with a runaway rocket! He said he would try to keep the Fire Marshal off my back and he gave me a ride home. Usually, after sessions with the State Police, I was stuck in Northampton and had to call a friend to come and get me.

I got at least one traffic ticket almost every month for crimes like exceeding the speed limit by one or two miles per hour. I spent many days in traffic court in South Hadley. Soon the traffic court judge recognized me and, discovering that I was being picked on, started to throw out the citations, and not a bit too soon. A few more citations would have caused the Registry of Motor Vehicles to suspend my license and registration. I still remember the names of the two police officers who would attack me any time they saw me traveling between Amherst and Northampton. I will now make them famous: Officers Wannat and Martula. Fortunately, my boss, Mr. Reuthier, was a very kind and decent man. My job was not in jeopardy. The police were trying to get me kicked out of my job so that I could be arrested for being an indigent with no means of support. This would have put me in prison for several years.

Soon I found that I would be ticketed for speeding even if I had not been driving an automobile! One time I drove to Quincy, about seventy miles away, to answer a traffic violation charge. I had never been in Quincy before in my life! I was sure that when I told the judge that there must be a mistake, he would apologize and let me go. I even brought a signed note from my boss stating that I was at his place of business for the entire day the offense was supposed to have happened.

It did no good. The judge sentenced me to a 100-dollar fine (or the House of Correction for ninety days). I did not have 100 dollars, but I was allowed a phone call. I called a friend who worked at the Hayden Inn and she loaned me the 100 dollars. By the time she arrived in Quincy to pay my fine, I had already been issued prison garb and was wearing handcuffs. Incidentally, a speeding charge in those days usually cost fifteen dollars.

I knew that I had to get out of the state of Massachusetts, or I would soon find myself in prison. This was the way it was in the sixties living in Massachusetts. The police did not just trample over the rights of blacks, but just about all young people as well. I was not an exception.

While working at the Television Center shop, I met several college professors from the university. I picked up a consulting job with one of them to make a timer for automatic microscopic photography. During my visits to the campus, I was quite surprised that a university could be such a nice place to live. The University of Massachusetts seemed quite a bit like Lyman School!

I studied very hard and took the test for the FCC first class commercial radio-telephone license. I passed it. Now I was qualified to work at radio and television stations. My first job at a radio station was at WARE in Ware. I had met another friend, Chris Payne, an amateur radio operator and the chief engineer of this station. After I helped him move the radio studio from an old building in the railway yard to a downtown location, he recommended me for his job and left to build a brand-new radio station, WTTT in Amherst. I lived at the transmitter site and even did some part-time work for Ed Belcher at the television shop.

Working at a radio station turned out to be a very good thing. The police no longer were picking on me, since they knew that anything unusual that might happen would be reported by the radio station. Our news radio reporter at WARE told me that when I first started at the station, the police chief told him that I was a firebug and that I would soon burn the radio station down. The reporter threatened to go on the air and tell everybody everything that the cop had said. The police chief decided to back off.

I became friends with a young police officer who used to eat his lunch in a restaurant across the street from the radio studio. He had been issued a photograph of me by the department and told that my movements were to be tracked just as with any other criminal. We had lunch together just about every day. Because of that, he knew me as a person, not some dangerous menace, and I liked him quite a lot as well. I told him what it was like at Lyman School. We also discussed my polygraph examinations at the State Police barracks. He said, "Damn! I never knew how they worked!" I never talked about the Youth Service Board.

I actually fulfilled my childhood dream of becoming a radio announcer, at least for a short while. Occasionally, I would have to pull an air shift, because the radio station maintained a directional antenna array in the nighttime and sometimes the deejay didn't show up for work. Radio stations that had directional antenna arrays needed to have a first class commercial radio operator licensee on duty. They were called "combo men." I was almost fired for a comment I made on the air: "Governor Peabody is the first governor of his state to have four towns named after him. They are Endicott, Peabody, Marblehead, and Athol!" I had not been aware that the tiny radio station, WARE, had such a far-reaching audience. The complaint came all the way from the governor's office. It seems like the new governor did not have a sense of humor.

My mother died the following year, stricken with cancer. She had been sick for a very long time. I was sorry that I never got a chance to tell her that I loved her. She made it very difficult. When I visited her in the hospital, she continued to curse me and blamed me for her cancer. She had truly been sick for a very long time. I felt a strange sort of relief when she died.

32

The Rest of the Story

During the next few years, I worked at several radio and television stations in Massachusetts. One of them was radio station WDEW in Westfield. That radio station owned a very old Western Electric radio transmitter that was always in need of repair. Its vacuum tubes, designed before World War II, were not available anymore. I convinced the manager of the station, Mr. Raymond Dowell, that I could design and build the radio station a new transmitter. Mr. Dowell then convinced the station owners to give me the go-ahead.

I am certain that it was one hell of an act of faith on the part of Mr. Dowell to let an eighteen-year-old attempt to design and build a radio transmitter for his radio station. I never let him down.

Within about six months I had constructed a modern one-kilowatt AM broadcast transmitter that worked like a charm and even looked very good. It used the latest technology. For instance, it did not have a crystal oven to keep its frequency-determining quartz crystal at a uniform temperature. Instead, it used a low-temperature coefficient device, housed in a glass envelope, made by Northern Engineering. The use of this device required a Federal Communications Commission (FCC) Rules change, which I got by proposing and documenting the new requested changes. I just telephoned the FCC Standards Bureau in Laurel, Maryland, asked to talk to the chief, and then did everything he told me to do.

The Federal Communications Commission required, of course, that the transmitter be type-accepted to comply with all the rules and regulations, just as though a company like RCA or Collins had supplied the transmitter. I was unable to make some of the tests and measurements required to comply with all of the rules, since I did not have some specialized test equipment, so the station hired a well-known consulting engineer, Dr. Don Howe.

Dr. Howe was Professor Emeritus at Worcester Polytechnic Institute. Working together, we certified the radio transmitter, which was listed in the FCC's list of approved equipment as the "Johnson Associates RBJ/1-C." Professor Howe helped me get into college some time later.

Interestingly, several famous persons had their start at radio station WDEW. Rich Wood, as a high school student who mowed the station's lawn, convinced the management that he could do an air shift on weekends. He became the Director of the WOR Network in New York and produced Tom Bodett's "End of the Road" program, the guy that does the commercials saying, "We'll keep the light on for you." Chris Payne had also worked at WDEW. He eventually worked on the AM Stereo project with Motorola and the National Association of Broadcasters. Ray Dowell went on to Chicago Radio and was the voice of Mr. Quinby in the Schweppes commercials. I was rubbing elbows with many famous people at that station!

REFLECTIONS

Mr. (Ray) Dowell asked me one day, when the radio transmitter was nearing completion, what it was that I wanted to do with my life. I told him that I wanted to complete the transmitter!

"No," he said, "what is it that you want to do later, after you've built the transmitter?"

I told him that I did not know. "As far as I know," I said, "finishing that transmitter is the most important thing that I could ever do." There would always be something else to do later.

You see, I never thought about the future, nor did I think about the past. I just devoted all my energies to the present task. The present task was building that radio transmitter. I wanted the transmitter to be perfect in every way possible. I spent many weeks stumbling over the mathematics of network equations. When I found a problem that I did not understand, I would go to the library and pore over many old textbooks in search of the answer.

For instance, the vacuum tube manufacturer specified a voltage and current for the output tubes. When I applied these values to the network equations, I was unable to arrive at the correct power output. Why was this so? The answer lies in the fact that the amplifier stage draws current in pulses, not steady-state values. The datasheets for the tubes were steady-state values. As a high school dropout, I learned about duty factor, conduction angle, and the mathematics of integration by parts.

I never knew any high school student who could perform numerical integration. That was something taught in college. I had to do better than a high school graduate did. The mathematics was important because I had to purchase some very expensive components for the output-tuning network. In amateur radio transmitters, one would just make everything variable and tune it. You cannot do this with a broadcast transmitter because it needs to have the correct bandwidth for high-fidelity audio and at the same time must comply with the FCC's spurious emissions criteria.

The transmitter was not perfect, but was good enough that Collins Radio, at the time the most respected radio transmitter company in the country, copied the design about a year after it was first published in the FCC Public Reference room and the transmitter went on the air. I always wanted to tell them that the last one-kilowatt transmitter that they designed, before they went out of the broadcast transmitter business, was a copy of a nineteen-year-old high school dropout's creation. So much for high tech.

Incidentally, in my subsequent career as an engineer, I acquired two patents and collaborated on several others. At an age when many engineers have changed careers to become real estate agents, I continue to lead a productive engineering career, designing software for high-speed, real-time applications. I continue to fly my airplane, and I have made two CD recordings of my piano music, one of them classical music and the other jazz. Although I have had to do some technical writing in my engineering career, this is my first book. I hope you have enjoyed it, and I hope it brings you closer to the understanding of why civilized society needs a place like the Lyman School, and why places like the Youth Service Board Detention Center must never again exist.

I find that as time goes by, there are subversive forces that continue to rewrite history. I have read dissertations referencing the Lyman School written by, in my opinion, persons who must have lived on a different planet. It is true that there were problems with the Lyman School for Boys, but instead of fixing those problems, the school was destroyed, leaving nowhere for the boys who needed its protection and services to go.

33

Back to School

Eventually I found myself on vacation while working at a union television station, WJZ-TV in Baltimore. With two weeks vacation on my hands and nothing to do, I decided to take the GED tests at the school board. I had never told anyone that I had never graduated from high school and, since I was a licensed professional, my supervisors probably assumed that I had. I thought that since I was now older than eighteen years of age, it was now legal for me to get an equivalency certificate. It would be nice to get the certificate just in case anybody ever asked. I took the test and it was easy.

A lady at the school board convinced me that, since the GEDs turned out to be so easy, I should take the college boards. She said, "You know, you've got a pretty good job at the television station, but they might even pay to send you to college if you do well in the tests." I told her I did not want to go to college, but I would take the tests anyway since I did not have anything else to do.

This lady at the school board became the first woman in my life. We eventually parted, and I do not know where she is now, so I will not use her name. She was an "older woman" who became my first love. She was twenty-six at the time!

I took the college board tests. They were not easy. I was sure that I flunked just about every subject in the tests. I do not know how it happened, but when I got the results (I scored in the nineties), I was sure that a mistake must have been made. I could not possibly have scored that high! Soon many colleges and universities were sending me literature, hoping I would enroll.

I was now nearly twenty-one years of age. The following autumn I started college. However, that is a completely different story.

Epilogue

Over forty years have passed. I have traveled to many countries in the world and lived in places near and far. Returning home, I come to the crest of a small hill. From here, I should see the Lyman School tower. There is nothing, not a sign of it! The tower is gone!

Off into the distance I search, trying to resolve the outline of majestic old Lyman Hall. For over two hundred years, I have been told, Lyman Hall had stood the test of time overlooking the valley between the shores of Lake Chauncey and Fay Mountain. It, too, is gone forever.

I drive through the main gate. Lyman School is closed. They have torn down my tower. Lyman Hall is gone. I can no longer hear the voices of the boys singing in the fields. Only the memories remain. Where do all the troubled boys go now? Who takes care of them? For so very many this was the only home they knew. This was where they found themselves, their true place in the human experience. It is no more.

I feel the loss, such an empty feeling. I expected to find bright young faces hard at work, some with grand expectations, working one day at a time building for tomorrow. I expected to see many changes, but I still believed I would see the continued purpose, a place where those who had traveled to the edge of hell would be hard at work to find again their place amongst the free, where each could work towards a better tomorrow.

However, Lyman School is gone. Perhaps there are no longer boys who need its help. Perhaps there are no longer troubled boys returning from hell in search of life. I suppose life is so much easier now. But suppose I am wrong.

A beech tree stands near Worcester Cottage. Beneath this tree, many boys sat and dreamed. They dreamed about the world beyond the horizon. They made plans for their future from this shaded spot. As I walk towards the tree, my legs start to weaken. I am walking on hallowed ground. I can feel the heartbeat of thousands who have stood on this spot before me. I kneel by the knees of the old beech tree. I feel so very much alone. Suddenly, I hear a voice: "I remember you from so very long ago. You were so very young and frail…"

Afterword

In this book, I have often related my personal affection for and relationship with Reverend F. Robert Brown, the Protestant chaplain during my stay at the Lyman School for Boys. One of the marvelous things he accomplished after I left the institution was to become Director of Training for the Commonwealth of Massachusetts Department of Youth Services. It is with great pride that I am presenting, with his permission, and in its entirety, one of Bob Brown's papers.

An Environment Fostering Choice—Peter's Story

Written for the
Department of Youth Services Training Program
Commonwealth of Massachusetts

By
F. Robert Brown
Director of Training (retired)

January 1998

INTRODUCTION

There are life stories that should be told, but the telling of such a life may produce so much pain and uneasiness that the telling would be unconscionable. That has been my dilemma over the last few years, but the passing of time has not removed the urgency which I feel to tell the story—a real life story.

The compromise I have made with myself is to tell the story being as factual as I can yet changing names and keeping hometowns and addresses blurry to protect the identity of the individual about whom I need to tell.

The events and times are true. The quotes are from the letters I treasure and keep. The locations of events are factual except, again, as it relates to hometown.

CHAPTER 1

Peter, after repeated arrests and juvenile court sessions, was committed to the Massachusetts Division of Youth Service and, because of his age, was sent to the Lyman School for Boys in the year 1960. Peter, a black youth, was large for his age but not an aggressive young man. His offenses stemmed mainly from a dysfunctional family situation where he was one of several siblings. There were school offenses and stubborn child complaints as well as some larceny charges.

His family residence was overcrowded and located in an area with high crime and delinquency. The housing unit was in need of repair. Winters were cold with little heat available in the apartment. Many nights of the year, Peter slept in the hallway because of overcrowding in the apartment.

At Lyman School, a state training school for delinquent boys, Peter was tested for educational class placement and termed uneducable and marginally retarded. He was placed in what was called the "special class," which pretty much meant he would never learn to read or write. During his stay at Lyman, he lived up to those expectations.

The Lyman School was the first training school ever built in the United States. In 1846, when the Commonwealth of Massachusetts decided to separate the youthful offender from the predominately adult prison system, the first building created was labeled a "reformatory." The label "reformatory" reflected the Commonwealth's concern that it was appropriate to separate the youthful offenders from the adult prison population, but there remained the concern that no reform should compromise the commitment to provide the maximum security necessary to protect the community from the youthful offenders. Therefore, the reformatory reflected the prison construction with cells, enclosed exercise yard, barred windows, and secure doors.

For twenty years, the reformatory housed all the male youthful offenders sentenced by the courts. Overcrowding, and the commingling of serious offenders with school offenders, stubborn children, and other less serious offenders produced a crisis which the Commonwealth sought to resolve by creating a new "treatment model" known as the Training School.

The Lyman School, located on a 500-acre tract of land adjacent to the reformatory, offered the space required to develop the Training School concept. It bore the name of one of the early reformers who had convinced the legislature that reform of the system was necessary, but who also helped fund new construction and endow its programs.

The Massachusetts Training School model housed the youth in separate cottages. These individual cottages were staffed by a husband and wife whose job it was to raise the family of youth placed in their cottage. The extensive grounds offered the room for large truck gardens, pastures, barns for livestock, fields to produce hay, and orchards for fruit.

The food needs were supplied onsite with the labor coming from the youth who attended school a half-day, and worked on the farm or other trades for the balance of the day. Other trades included a blacksmith shop, carpentry shop, plumbing and electrical shops, the laundry, an institutional kitchen, a print shop, and a maintenance crew.

Recreation provisions comprised ball fields, basketball courts, an inside gym and swimming pool, a roller-skating rink, and a movie theater. Church attendance was mandatory for all youth and each boy had a special suit or sport coat, which he wore to church and other special occasions.

When Peter was at the Lyman School, it was housing nearly 500 boys in a bed capacity of 320. The cottage populations were exploding and the state was losing the capacity to find husband and wife teams willing to work 24 hours per day, 7 days a week. As a result, additional staff was required to cover shifts in the cottages, thus corrupting the original family concept. Still, in spite of deteriorating conditions, the emphasis on security, safety, and care was based upon relationships between staff and youth.

The first institution carried that arrogant title, "Reformatory." Not only is the title arrogant, but also contradictory. Society has always sought to separate the law-abiding citizen from the offender, and especially, the most violent of the offenders. The construction, which helped assure that separation, was the prison. As castles and forts built walls and buttresses to protect those inside from invasion and harm from the outside, the prison built walls and buttresses to pen-up and control the inmate inside.

As more thought and new technologies allowed, security was constantly increased to insure that escapes would be minimized. However, any thinking society was aware that, in time, most offenders would be returning to the community, so there was concern that rehabilitation also takes place.

The title, "Reformatory" reflects that concern. What makes this title contradictory is that the emphasis on security so isolated the inmate that he could experience nothing of the realities of living in a community. Rather than allowing the incarcerated to become constructively independent, the regime of institutional living made them completely dependent upon the instructional daily routine, which was repetitious and orchestrated by the clock. Individuals (inmates) learned simply to respond to orders and rarely think or plan for themselves. Every detail was taken care of, from what clothes to wear, when one got up, when one slept, what one ate, and what one did all day long.

Therefore, the environment was completely inconsistent with fostering a rehabilitation model where inmates could learn to become constructive citizens. Fear of independence forced dependence, and thus when the doors were finally thrown open for the inmate, it was often not long before he was back. He was back because he simply could not survive in a world where he had no idea about how to get or hold a job, find or pay for an apartment, buy or prepare food, or handle the other problems of living on the outside.

The title, "Reformatory" was arrogant because it says rather bluntly, "We will fix you." To be sure, the institutional routine broke street behaviors instantly. The support group (gang or peers) was removed, the weapons were gone, the familiar surroundings were changed, and others controlled the youth's life instantly. Misbehavior had distasteful consequences, so one learned how to behave quickly.

Many interpreted that to be the power of rehabilitation. The power of the correctional system left the impression that the institution could reform the inmate. However, the historical truth is that, though dependence grew, few new and positive values or skills were developed to support the inmate and his reentry into the community.

The truth is no human being or system can make a person change if the person does not want to. What does happen is that the inmate adapts to the environment and chooses to play the game, the game necessary to get out. Because it is a game, not a commitment to change, life on the street remains the same, and soon the individual is in trouble again. The old behaviors are resumed and the same old values lived.

The Training School, though far from perfect, offered more that was conducive to a positive rehabilitation model. The Training School used the concept that good families produce good kids and poor families produce troubled kids. The treatment goal was to create a good family into which was inserted poorly acting youth. The premise and hope was that the positive family model would create the environment where change in behavior would take place primarily because the youth chose to change.

In the early days, the working habits of the couples employed allowed for the perfect family model for each couple lived as fulltime residents in their home and lived as a family does in constant relationship with the children. As the years passed, and labor habits changed, the family model gave way to additional staff working in shifts. However, as noted earlier, the emphasis remained on relationships between youth and staff.

As the community grew, because of the ever-increasing numbers of youth being sent by the courts, additional staff and programs were added. Teachers, counselors, trade instructors, recreation people, farmers, tradesmen, and chaplains became permanent staff members.

To the casual observer, the Training School looked more like a prep school than a correctional institution. The sprawling campus of individual cottages, administration building, infirmary, cafeteria, school, chaplains' office building, and the farm occupied over 100 acres with an additional 400 acres of farmland and open space for ball fields, playgrounds, basketball courts, and gardens spread over a gentle hill. This hardly left the impression of a correctional institution.

No security fences, guards, or patrols existed. The Training School was an open model with security based solely upon the relationships created between youth and staff and the vigilance of staff that could sense unrest and crises, which usually predicted runaways. In the early days, there was an interesting way of alerting the community if any of the youths ran away. It was a steam whistle on the roof of the power plant, which blew a shrill warning. It was the tradition for any who heard the whistle, and who wished to enter the chase, to be on the lookout for the runaway. If found and apprehended by the local citizen, a bounty was paid for the youth's capture.

Although there were runaways, it is rather remarkable that so many young people could be sent to the training school against their will and could be kept in the institution without the normal tools of security. The secret comes back to the quality of life, which good staff and appropriate programs were able to create, and that is reflected in the different title for the institution.

The first institution was called the Reformatory. We have discussed the implications of that title. The Training School was a less arrogant concept because the treatment model directed itself more to the remedial aspects of providing youth with the opportunity for individual relationships with a caring staff. The family model was almost ideal, but even after that model became impractical, the emphasis upon small groups (the cottage) and the relationships with staff still produced an environment in which some interesting change could and did take place.

For those of us who worked in that environment, it quietly dawned upon us that our mission was to create an environment in which a now delinquent youth could choose to become nondelinquent. That goal or mission never was formalized by the system as a mission statement, probably because it was not consistent with the political demands of the time, which would have winced at any concept, which did not brag that it could change a youth's behavior. Yet my reflection is that is exactly what we were doing, and it clearly defined our role and conduct as staff.

What I did as a Chaplain that was right or wrong in working with youth could be criticized and evaluated by asking the question, "Did I positively or negatively impact the environment where a youth could choose to become nondelinquent?" The key ingredients in creating an environment in which delinquent youth would choose to become nondelinquent, were, and are, fine male and female staff. Those staff who chose to work with very difficult, demanding, testing, untrusting, and often untruthful youth and did not personalize negative behavior directed at them during the testing process were the most successful at working with the youth.

The young people, who found committed, caring, staff at the training school, saw them as an oddity and often questioned why one would choose to work with them. Nevertheless, when the testing process was over, and the bonding of relationship began, one would often see the often subtle reflections of that bond of respect. Patterns of speech, clothes worn, hairstyles on the part of the youth, often began to look like the "Master" who cared for them most consistently.

Boys often asked staff if they could come and live with them or if the staff person could become their mom or dad. As a Chaplain, I often heard boys say that they wanted to live like a particular staff member whom they especially respected.

A second ingredient of the environment where a youth could choose to become nondelinquent was the recognition of each youth as a separate and distinct individual. A major criticism of large institutional settings has always been that they are so impersonal. It was the commitment of good staff to know and respect each youth as a separate and distinct individual, which broke the institutional, herd mentality. The staff person who quickly leaned the youth's name rather than calling, "Hey, you come over here," and took the time to speak to each youth in his or her care every day soon became precious in the sight of a frightened young person.

In knowing each youth, one quickly began to see how much of a con game each youth had to live with, in order to be an equal among his peers. The tough exterior of so many youth was paper-thin and quickly disappeared when caring staff offered acceptance of them as individuals. I have hosted many tearful sessions behind closed doors when the young person was not being watched by his peers, he could let his real fears and vulnerabilities show.

So many youth who carry the label of delinquent have rarely experienced the attention necessary from caring adults, which let them know they are valued. The mere fact that staff knew their name and talked to them as individuals, had a tremendous impact on creating an environment where youth felt accepted and where they could begin to build a positive ego.

The third element of an environment in which a delinquent youth could choose to become nondelinquent is that which dictates that the daily program be relevant to the needs of the youth. The proper grade placement in school and vocational training which related to the job aspirations of a youth, or options for jobs that allowed a youth to explore different kinds of career options, are examples of relevant programming.

Individual and group counseling directed at demonstrated needs of youth such as drug and alcohol addiction, sex offending, violence prevention, etc., are further examples of daily programming designed to meet the needs of youth. When the youth felt that the daily program was relevant to his needs, youth tended to invest in it and use the time away from home more constructively.

The general perception of institutional life was that little attention was given to individuals, and most of the institutional life was based upon the herd approach, i.e., everybody doing the same thing and all being treated the same. However, the reality of The Lyman School for Boys was that, in spite of large populations, there were many dedicated and committed staff who took the time to be sure each boy received individual attention and attempted to match the youth to the program ingredients most relevant to his needs.

The story of Peter's life is a validation of the concept that juvenile justice systems, when properly constructed, can create environments where delinquent youth can choose to be nondelinquent and more.

There is a reality, however, that change often takes more time to become fixed as a new persona than is allowed in a juvenile system where youth generally leave before the chosen change in their life is completed. In a sense, then, the system often is like a farm hothouse where seedbeds are prepared, seeds are planted, and the temperature, moisture, and sunlight are properly controlled. One hopes that the seeds will properly germinate and show signs of being healthy plants as it becomes time to set them out. As the youth leave the system, they are like the plant being set out in the field. More development and growth is needed before the plant or young man matures to bear fruit.

CHAPTER 2

During the days Peter was at the training school, the Vietnam War was developing and the military was recruiting young men wherever they could. As time went on, the recruiters found the training school and eagerly recruited almost any young man who was old enough and willing to sign up. Peter elected to join the Army.

Peter had grown to be a big boy. His size acted as a deterrent to those who might choose to pick a fight with him. Yet Peter was a gentle, sensitive young man when he dared to show that side of his personality. Although he was a black youth and I was white, Peter was one of the most accepting young men I had ever met. He seemed to have no sense of prejudice. He trusted and showed respect for the adults with whom he came in contact. Though others might show him prejudice, he always seemed to be able to rise above it.

Peter and I had had a very friendly, open relationship while he was at the Lyman School. Though he had no choice about attending church (it was compulsory in those days), Peter often asked questions about something I had said in the sermon or was interested in the power of prayer.

Every young man who came to the Lyman School and who was not a Catholic was considered a Protestant. When I met each young man for the first time, it was my practice to give each young man a Bible provided by the Massachusetts Bible Society and a little medal which they hung around their neck which had a head of Jesus and the words, "I am a Protestant" on it. I gave the medals because the Catholic boys all had medals and chains, which were often stolen by the Protestant boys. Therefore, if all the boys had medals, there was less conflict and combat.

Many years after he left the institution, Peter told me he still had his Bible and medal. Peter and I had a relationship, which developed to a new level when he completed his basic Army training, and was sent to Vietnam. We corresponded regularly. I have kept every letter Peter sent me. I have marveled at the growth of his character. I share some of these treasured letters with you as one who "stands in awe" of the courage, loyalty, compassion, and class of this "non-delinquent" man.

I often used to ask boys what they planned to be doing when they were thirty years old. The usual response from the boys who rarely saw any future for themselves was either a quizzical look or the statement that they never expected to be alive at thirty. Thirty was an old age and not an age that they expected to see. The further implication was that their life had no value, they had nothing to offer in life, and this life was so negative that they wanted out. This clearly accounts for the alarming number of attempted and successful suicides among this population.

With that as background, I was always interested in the initials that appeared on the outside of every envelope which carried Peter's letters. The letters were, "O W T, N M." Peter never made any mention about what those letters stood for, and I never asked. However, one day the letter came with the words rather than the letters. The words put a chill up my spine, "One way ticket, not me." Peter had not gone to Vietnam to die. Though enmeshed in the heart of the battles, Peter intended to come home.

As noted earlier, Peter had been tested and classified as uneducable by the school system in the training school. He was placed in what was called a special class. While at the training school, he retained a very limited ability to read and write. The onset of letters surprised me because they were carefully written, and often answered questions which I had written in letters to him. Not only had he become a competent soldier but also he dramatically improved his communications skills. Peter was far from the "dummy" which he had been labeled in the training school.

In 1966 the letters started. The war was beginning its third year in 1966 when Peter began his first tour. The number of US troops was growing rapidly. At the start of the year, there were 184,300 U.S. troops on Vietnamese soil. By the end of the year, the force had grown to 385,300.

Peter was part of the "1st Air Calvary Division" which was deployed in the center of South Vietnam in a critical spot. The North Vietnamese had calculated to penetrate in this part of the South to be able to cut it in half and thus isolate the armed forces in South Vietnam. One of the towns in this section was the town of AnKhe, which Peter will talk about in later letters.

Early in Peter's stay, he was involved in what was eventually described as an accidental shooting of a fellow soldier. For a time, it looked as if he would be found guilty of an offense, and it looked as if he would be prosecuted.

Dear Rev. Brown,

I hope this letter finds you and yours in the best of health, and also the rest of the boys there at Lyman. Well, Rev. I guess you must be wondering why I am writing. Well the truth is that I am in trouble again.

You see, Rev, I shot a good friend of mine when we were on our last field problem. It was an accident but my company commander is out for me and he is trying to give me a court marshal on the grounds that it was intentional so I told him that this is one time that we are going to go all the way so that if we have to take it to the supreme court and I kid you not.

Things got so bad that I cut my wrist because I just cant take any more of this so called Army. But I know now that I can not kill any man but the Army told me that they don't care what I think so I guess if I go out in the field and get a whole bunch of good G.I.s killed because I cant kill them they tell me that I am a coward, but Rev. all I know is that I cant kill because it would drive me nuts just knowing that I killed a man.

The man I shot his name is Vito and I cant even get him off my mind, It got so bad just thinking that I could have killed him that I tried killing myself.

Rev. I dont want to hurt people all I want to do is help them. I asked if I could go to work for the Red Cross and they told me no.

I wrote a letter to the president Mr. Johnson but I dont if he will understand the way I feel so I was wondering if you could write him and let him know how I feel and ask him if I could go to work for the Red Cross and help people and not kill them. You are the only person that I can turn to Rev. for when I was at Lyman you use to help me write letters and now I need your help more than ever. I pray to God for help but things just get worse and the next time I try cutting my wrist it will be for good for I don't want to hurt people all I want to do is help and I would rather take my own life. I tried once but the next time I will make it.

So please Rev. Write and ask the president if I can help and not kill people.

One of your boys,

Peter

Eventually, however, the inquiry determined that it was an accident and he was cleared. However, the event had caused him a great deal of emotional trauma. Not only did he have to deal with the accident, but also he began his struggle with the whole issue of life and death within the context of a complex war situation.

I was desperate to know how to help him. I was not sure I would have any better result in writing to the President though I did because of his request. I also began to track down an Army Chaplain who might be able to help him.

I was fortunate to be able to contact Chaplain Major Richard Hartman who quickly acted upon my request that Peter be seen and helped. I was deeply relieved to get this note from Chaplain Hartman.

> *Received your letter regarding Peter and would like to express my appreciation for your concern. I have talked with him more than once and am fully aware of his present problem.*
>
> *First of all, he is not going to be court-martialed, but has been transferred to another unit in order to give him every opportunity to do a job. I believe he is doing much better now…*

One of the proudest days of his life and mine was his promotion to the rank of Sergeant. He had reestablished his reputation as a reliable soldier, and begun to demonstrate a competency recognized by those living with him in the battle arena. A letter arrived one day, which had a different feel to it. In it was a lump, which I felt as soon as I picked it up. As I opened it, the lump revealed itself. That lump produced more than a lump in my throat. I was deeply moved as I held it in my hand, his Sergeant stripe on which he had written, "To a good friend."

What an incredible gift! This was further validation of the concept that young people can choose to be nondelinquent and can achieve even in a competitive world. The letters and the war continued, so did the moral development of a remarkable young man.

At a point in the war in May of 1966, this letter arrived.

> *Well to tell the truth things are kind of bad over here but they could be ruffer if you know what I mean. The CAV is doing one H—of a job over here and don't let anyone kid you, they are paying the price of victory and if you ask me the price of victory is H—. We have a saying over here and it goes like this (when I die I must go to heaven, for I have spent my time in H—). In your letter you asked me what you could send me. Well Rev, to tell the truth I dont need anything. A plane ticket home maybe (smile) but the people over here could use anything you and the school could send like soap, close, toothbrushes and etc.*
>
> *You know Rev there are few things that move me, but to see the way these people live does just that (move me) you know I use to think that I had it bad when I*

was at the school and home, but now I thank God that he was aloud me to live the way I have. You know Im not one for ideas but I was just thinking, if you could start a drive or something at your church and ask the people if they had any old things that they could no longer use, and if you told them what it was for and I think they would come a cross as the saying go's.

Rev. Brown, I don't believe that all these people are V.C. for I cant take two hundred people and say they are all V.C. for I don't know if the people back home know this or not, but the people over here are starting to realize the G.I. is here to help and not to hurt, and the V.C. are losing their foot hold that they had on the people, for they know we are here to help and I have always believed that if you show people that you mean to help them they will in return help you and in doing so will help themselves.

Pay day when I get paid I will by some film and take some pictures of the town of An-Khe and of the people. Just so the people back home can see what it is like to live in H—and to see people suffer. So Rev I think if you will tell the people what I have told you I think then will understand (don't you).

And if they should ask why are our boys dieing over their tell them this. Love of God and country is not be question. For no man wants to die and that go's for me as well as the next man, but ask them this would they give up their freedom without a fight. I dont think so. I know I would not.

I believe that every G.I. over here knows it is wrong to kill his fellow man, but to defeat a tirent is to help God. and this I believe with all my heart and soul. I shot a friend of mine and I crocked and I said that I would never kill but I was only kidding myself. For if I saw a friend under fire I think I would go to his aid. So Rev. Brown we over here need the help of the people back home to help end this war so what have we got to lose by asking the people (you tell me) (smile). And I think the people back home will come across. And tell that they can get into the fight and help end this war if they will only send what they can. I know my spelling is bad but you know me (smile) and beside I think you know what I am saying or trying to say. Well Rev I guess this is it for now, but please tell the boys at the school this for me.

If the G.I.s end this war soon and they will, that they will not have to worry about coming over here. And also tell them this. They should not feel ashamed of being at the school if it is going to do them any good. And they are the only one's that know the answer to that. For it took me four times at the school to set me straight, but I hope they will not have to learn that way. For all they have to do is tell themselves no when they are going to do something wrong. I told myself no the last time I was there and I have not been back to spend anymore time and tell them of the few of the things I have facing me and what happened to me since Ive been over here and I doubt if their problems will even come close to mine. For I feel that the road is not yet ironed out yet, but I am not about to give up yet and I doubt very much I will.

Well Rev I think I have said abut all I can say only life is a hard game to play and if you play by the rules you will win in the end and you must believe in the man above, and it took a place like this to get me baptized and if I have to fight to keep going I will do so.

So my closing words are this. May God bless you and yours and the boys and thanks for everything.

While Peter was struggling in Vietnam, life went on back at the Lyman School. Our routines continued. One part of that routine was our weekly worship service held in the auditorium. This was a compulsory service, but one of the rare times in the life of the school where the boys were left to control their own behavior because the Cottage Masters and other staff needed to remain with the Catholic boys while the Protestants were at church.

So it was I, as the Chaplain, and organist and one staff, stationed by the phone to maintain communication if needed, who supervised over 100 boys.

Our services consisted of prayers, hymn singing, Scripture readings, a sermon, and a benediction. Soon after Peter's letters started to come, I would spend a few minutes telling the boys about where Peter was and what was going on in this area of the war. There was complete attention when I talked about Peter. They were hearing about the war every day. They were also hearing about peace rallies and an increasingly violent response by the peaceniks objecting to the war. They heard the names being thrown at veterans returning. These were very difficult and confusing times for these young people.

When the letters came describing the orphanage and the town of AnKhe the boys really took special notice. I had no real sense of what they were feeling until one Sunday morning, just after I read the latest letter, one of the boys very politely stood up, not to interrupt the service, but to respond emotionally to what he was feeling.

His initial remarks were simple a question, "Rev, can we help?" He caught me off guard. Before I could answer one of his buddies also stood up and said, "Rev, we go on weekends and we have visits from parents. We have other visitors who could ask for help. Rev, if you do not ask where we are getting the stuff, we will get things for Peter to give to the orphanage and the village people."

My mind raced. Here I stood in my robe in the midst of a worship being challenged with a real moral dilemma. I make no value judgment as to whether I did the right thing or not, but my answer was, "I will accept anything you can bring me for Peter as long as you pledge not to hurt anyone to get it."

There was a little titter of nervous laughter throughout the congregation, but the deal was made. The collection began. As the days went by, we had gathered enough diapers, food, clothing, soap, etc., for us to send many huge boxes to Peter.

Peter was overwhelmed by the boys' efforts. He got so much stuff over the time that he was in that area that he was able to not only adopt an orphanage, but also the whole town of AnKhe.

The military newspaper picked up on what was happening and took pictures of Peter and his buddies distributing the goods to the kids. For possibly the first time in his life, Peter was a "celebrity" being photographed and written about as he performed this humanitarian act.

What a thrill it was for me to see Peter who, though thrust on to the battlefield to kill, was also being directed by his heart to love and care for others caught up in the suffering of war.

The magnitude of what he was experiencing was made especially poignant for me when he wrote, "I never knew how good I had it until I saw this orphanage." I know of the difficult family and living conditions he had survived, and by American standards, they were deplorable. Now he reflects that he had it "pretty good" when compared with the suffering he was now seeing. This was certainly substance for the phrase he once wrote, "…war is hell."

A letter in November of 1966 spoke of his feelings at that time.

> *I received 8 packages last night and tomorrow I morning I will take them in to town to the orphanage. I have some slide film ads if one of the fellas will let me used his camera I hope to take some pictures so that the boys at the school can get a first hand idea of the wonderful job they are doing.*

> *You know Rev. Brown a lot of people use a lot of words to try and say or explain something they want to say. I truly believe that there are not enough words to explain the wonderful thing that the boys and staff at the school are doing. Something kind of wonderful happened three weeks ago. Remember the last package you sent? Well the chaplain…Chaplain Wright, called the radio station here at base camp, and they sent some people with us to where the packages were taken.*

They had me on the radio station and they also took some pictures. I was told the pictures would be put in the D.I.V. newspaper with the story that the boys at the school were doing.

I have a lot of people come up to me and tell me what a wonderful job they think the boys and staff at the school are doing. It really makes me feel dam good to know that there are people like the people that I am working with to try and bring a little happiness into someone's life that is less fortunate and all I can really say is God bless and take care of yours.

Peter served three tours in Vietnam. Though he never made much of the reason for volunteering for an additional tour, I know he did so, so that one of his brothers did not have to go. He and two of his brothers served, and he thought that was enough and expressed it when he wrote, "My mother thinks her whole family is being asked to die for Uncle Sam."

The reality of war was always present in his life. In December of 1966, he wrote:

In my last letter I asked if I might have a picture of the school grounds. I dont know why, but I always did like the way the school looked after a heavy snow. Maybe Im just some kind of a sentimentalist.

We are still in the field and from the looks of things we may be out here until the end of March. I dont know if you heard the news on T.V. or radio yet, but on the 17th of this month the 1st of the 8th CAV ran into what they thought was a company of V.C. It turned out to be two Br. of V.C. things really got bad. The CAV really did a fine job, but the price they paid was not worth the win of the battle if you ask me.

My unit is set up right across from the 15th MED-A-VAC hospital and some of the things we see can really put one in a state. You could tell from the looks of the dead that they never knew what hit them. I have seen this many times before but each time is like seeing it for the first. You never get use to seeing it. and a lot of these men only had about 20 days left. I tell you Rev if I ever get it or make the last mail call as we say over here, I hope its neat and fast.

Well Rev Brown I really must go. So do us both a small favor. Have a Merry Christmas and a Happy New Year for the both of us (smile) take care and may God bless you and yours.

Between one of his tours Peter was able to come home. He wrote me that he would be home at a particular time and he asked if he could come and visit the school.

I was thrilled at the prospect of seeing him again and told the boys during one of the church services. They too were excited. As word traveled throughout the Lyman School, we began to make plans for his visit. He had indicated to me that he would like to wander the grounds and drop in to see the staff he liked while at school. Therefore, it was decided that I would escort him around and we would change the institution routine to celebrate his homecoming—and it was really a homecoming.

Peter often said that the Lyman School was there when he needed it and he really looked at it as a home where he had experienced love, direction, and support. In spite of the institution failings, the good outweighed the negative for him.

To show how much we loved him, and how eager we were to see him, we cancelled all the normal programs and brought all the staff and youth together in the auditorium. The plan was that at the right time, I would guide him to the auditorium which we had blackened (turned off all the lights, and closed the shutters on the windows), and all the youth and staff would be "absolutely quiet."

Peter arrived in his dress uniform with his Sergeant stripes proudly sewn in place, his uniform carefully pressed, and his shoes spit shined. What a sight! I cried when I saw him and our embrace nearly stained his uniform with mutual tears. I immediately had to start making excuses for the seeming absence of the office staff and administrators, but I suggested we start our walk around the campus where we could see the folks he wanted to see.

The administration building was near the highway with the rest of the campus expanding as one climbed the hill from the AB building. The second building up the road was the auditorium, which was used for movies on Saturday and church on Sunday. As we approached the auditorium, Peter mused that he remembered going to church and asked if it still looked the same. I said it did but asked, "Do you want to stop in?" He did.

We walked to the door and I moved ahead to open it for him. He entered first. The huge room was dark and silent. He took about four steps into the dark chasm when as perfectly programmed, the lights were thrown on, and the whole throng—about 300 young people and 30 or so staff—jumped to their feet and gave him an incredible standing ovation.

I thought he would collapse. Through a torrent of tears flowing from my eyes, I watched him be overwhelmed, but he recovered and with real grace moved to the front of the auditorium. With no preparation, he gave an eloquent talk about the war, his role, the problem with the peace movement, AnKhe, and ended with a hearty thanks to the kids and staff for their help, for sending packages, and for this grand welcome home.

He also invited the boys to write him and he promised that as his duties of being involved in the fighting of the war allowed, he would answer each letter. In the days that followed, Peter returned to Vietnam and fulfilled his promise.

Many times boys at the school would come running down to my office to show me their latest letter from Peter. The letters were as if from a loving, older brother who tried to respond in honesty to all the questions asked but always included a message that Peter believed they would become good citizens if they continued to work hard at improving those necessary life skills provided by the school and church.

After returning to Vietnam for his next tour, this letter came.

Dear Rev. Brown,

Just a few lines to let you know that I received your letters and packages. The Chaplain also received the packages you and the boys sent and for them we want to thank you all.

Rev. Brown, you think the boys were impressed. Well I was the one that was impressed more than anyone. To meet and know the young men who are so willing to give a helping hand to people who need the help of people like the young men at the school.

You know Rev. Brown, it really made me feel good to meet those young men and please tell them for me, thank you for a job well done.

You know Rev Brown I doubt very much that you will see most of those young men again for I dont believe that young men like those at the school now will return for I feel that they know the job that they are doing for the people over hear in VietNam is a job that must be done. And this alone has made them men in my way of thinking.

I am sorry that it has taken me so long to answer your letter, but the day I got back I had to go to the field. I got back to Viet Nam on the 9th of September and the same day I had to go back to the field, and that night we got hit. We lost two men in B. Btry and I thank God that it was not more.

You know it feels kind of odd to have gone home where there is no war going on and then come back to this hell hole and wonder if you are going to leave the same way you came. But like I told the boys, I have a job to do and it will be done even if I die trying. For I know in my heart that the job will go on and with young men like those in the school I know the job will be done.

Well Rev. I have to go now, but in closing I would like to say thank you and may God bless you all.

The war continued, Peter wrote in April 1968.

Well this new assignment of mine is not the best in the Army, but like they say, all is fair in love and war. This place that I am at is the delta of Nam. The town of Soctrang is not a very bad place, but like I always say it could be better.

Tonight I have bunker guard. On the way to the bunker I saw one of our gunships shooting out over the perimeter. This is something one gets use to seeing just about every night. The only thing that might bother you is when you see tracers going up instead of down.

About three nights ago we really had a fight. It seems that (Sir Charles) had a minie gun and he did bring a little smoke on the gunships, but none of the gunners were killed. We got mortared about three to four times a month. Most of the time they waite till about 2 or 3 in the morning and whamo! All hell brakes loose.

I remember when (Sir Charles) had a big push on over here a few month ago. We got hit for 10 days straight. What made it hot was that all we could do was sit here and take it. We had 14 men killed. I had told one of those men to keep his head down and he said no bullets had his name on them. Not an hour later this same man was dead.

I have learned about the killing of Dr. King. Really wonder what next. All the killing and fighting that followed his death dose not pay much tribute to his death. All things take time, but what will all this prove? They say only the good die young. I guess never has a saying been more true. My brother is here in Soctrang with me. I asked him what he thought about the whole thing. He just looked at me gave a slight grin and said keep the faith baby. I guess he is right. For in this time when all faith is needed we must keep the faith in God and even more so country.

I still have that feeling that it will all work out. You and I may not be around to see it, but it will come some day.

CHAPTER 3

It always amazed me that Peter was so willing to reach out when it would have been so easy and logical for Peter to be looking for people to support and care for him especially when I allow myself to try to picture the "hell" he knew each day.

Peter knew that any day could be his last. He was constantly within the sights and sounds of war. He had seen too many body bags and maimed comrades not to know how fragile life was. Nevertheless, each letter I received from his always carried the initials, OWT, NM, or the words, "One way ticket, not me." He intended to live and refused to let himself dwell on a fear of death.

I marveled then and still do to this day, from where did that will to live come? Where did his determination to serve his country and his fellow man come from?

Peter, by so many measures was a born loser. He was not blessed with an intact, supporting family. He knew only poverty and difficult living conditions. He was misread by so many social work types in his life. He was labeled uneducable and suspected of being retarded. He knew prejudice and lived through the battlefield experience in Vietnam, but also experienced first hand the national rejection and contempt heaped upon our soldiers by a misguided, ungrateful nation. Yet he willed to live and truly seemed to find his greatest happiness and feeling of worth in his service to others.

I leave the answers to those questions to you. Let me simply suggest that our task as workers with youth is to create an environment where youth can choose to be all that God intended for them to be. We do not make the choice nor force the change. We simply create the environment of support and caring which allows that choice to be made and nurtured.

When you are privileged to be able to watch it happen, the chance Peter gave me, you too will stand back in humbleness and awe quietly thanking your God that he allowed you to play a small part and be witness to the miracle of change. If you are caught up in it as I did, you will find your life hero. For me, my hero is Peter to whom I will be eternally grateful for all he taught about courage, caring, determination, grit, loving, and class.

Dear Peter,
Thank You!

978-0-595-38667
0-595-38667-9